First World War
and Army of Occupation
War Diary
France, Belgium and Germany

21 DIVISION
63 Infantry Brigade
Duke of Cambridge's Own (Middlesex Regiment)
4th Battalion
1 November 1915 - 30 June 1916

WO95/2158/2

The Naval & Military Press Ltd
www.nmarchive.com
Published in association with The National Archives

Published by

The Naval & Military Press Ltd

Unit 10 Ridgewood Industrial Park,

Uckfield, East Sussex,

TN22 5QE England

Tel: +44 (0) 1825 749494

www.naval-military-press.com

www.nmarchive.com

This diary has been reprinted in facsimile from the original. Any imperfections are inevitably reproduced and the quality may fall short of modern type and cartographic standards.

© Crown Copyright
Images reproduced by permission of The National Archives, London, England, 2015.

Contents

Document type	Place/Title	Date From	Date To
Heading	WO95/2158/2		
Heading	21st Division 63rd Infy Bde 4th Bn Middlesex Regt Nov 1915-Jun 1916 From 3 Div 8 Bde To 37 Div 63 Bde		
Heading	21st Division Transferred Nov 4th Middx Nov Vol XVI		
War Diary	Steenvorde	01/11/1915	12/11/1915
War Diary	Steenvoorde to Bailleul	13/11/1915	13/11/1915
War Diary	Bailleul to Armentiers	14/11/1915	14/11/1915
War Diary	Armentieres	15/11/1915	30/11/1915
Heading	21st Div 4/M'sex Rgt. Dec 1915 Vol. XVII		
War Diary	Armentiers	01/12/1915	31/12/1915
Heading	21st Div 4th Middlesex Regt Jan Vol. XVIII		
War Diary	Armentiers	01/01/1916	31/01/1916
Diagram etc			
War Diary	Armentiers	01/02/1916	29/02/1916
Diagram etc	Enemy Line Brune Rue		
Heading	4 Middlesex Regt Vol XX		
War Diary	Armentiers	01/03/1916	08/03/1916
War Diary		08/03/1916	11/03/1916
War Diary	Armentiers	11/03/1916	21/03/1916
War Diary	Strazeele	21/03/1916	31/03/1916
Heading	3/21 Middlesex Regt Vol XIX		
War Diary	Amiens	01/04/1916	01/04/1916
War Diary	Allonville	02/04/1916	03/04/1916
War Diary	Allonville Near Amiens	04/04/1916	06/04/1916
War Diary	Allonville	07/04/1916	07/04/1916
War Diary	Ville	08/04/1916	14/04/1916
War Diary	Trenches Near Meault & Fricourt	14/04/1916	23/04/1916
War Diary	La Neuville	24/04/1916	30/04/1916
Diagram etc	Sketch Shewing Battalion Front		
War Diary	La Neuville	01/05/1916	02/05/1916
War Diary	Ville	03/05/1916	04/05/1916
War Diary	Ville Sur Somme	05/05/1916	11/05/1916
War Diary	Fricourt Sector	12/05/1916	22/05/1916
War Diary	Buire	23/05/1916	23/05/1916
War Diary	La Neuville	23/05/1916	31/05/1916
Miscellaneous	Operation Order By Lieut-Colonel H.P.F. Bicknell, D.S.O. Commanding, 4th Battalion Middlesex Regiment.		
War Diary	Meaulte	01/06/1916	10/06/1916
War Diary	Fricourt Sector	11/06/1916	16/06/1916
War Diary	Meaulte	17/06/1916	20/06/1916
War Diary	La Neuville	21/06/1916	26/06/1916
War Diary	Ville	27/06/1916	27/06/1916
War Diary	Left Sector	28/06/1916	28/06/1916
War Diary	Queen's Robert	29/06/1916	29/06/1916
War Diary	Left Sector	30/06/1916	30/06/1916
Miscellaneous	Re L/Cpl Burgess Reported Missing, 14th Inst.	16/06/1916	16/06/1916

woas/2/2b00 28258

21ST DIVISION
63RD INFY BDE

4TH BN MIDDLESEX REGT
NOV 1915 - JUN 1916

FROM 3 DIV 8 BDE
TO 37 DIV 63 BDE

21ST DIVISION
63RD INFY BDE

63/21

4ta M'aava
2002
Loe XVI

12/
7655

21st 3/40 Ivan

Transferred Nov 14th 144

Army Form C. 2118

WAR DIARY
or
INTELLIGENCE SUMMARY
(Erase heading not required.)

Instructions regarding War Diaries and Intelligence Summaries are contained in F. S. Regs., Part II. and the Staff Manual respectively. Title Pages will be prepared in manuscript.

Place	Date	Hour	Summary of Events and Information	Remarks and references to Appendices
STEENVORDE	1/7/15		Batt. Resting, usual classes continued. Weather inclement. Silent Parade returned from Brewer tennis tent over Br Brennan	TBW
	2/7/15		Batt. Resting usual classes continued. Lt Robinson proceeds to Boulogne tribunal. Tournament went on there.	TBW
	3/7/15		Batt. Resting Rain stopped work, return unknown. Capt Hurley, Lt Fry amongst them.	TBW
	4/7/15		Batt. Resting. Usual classes continuing.	
	5/7/15		Resting. Capt Hoher, Lt Jeffreys & Lt Parsons 2nd Cos wounded at Grenville Dressing Station at VLAMDINGHE M See 7/3/	
	6/7/15		were evacuated. Church Parades as usual.	TBW
	7/7/15			
	7/7/15		Batt. resting. No especial events. Several Company	
	8/7/15		football matches played.	TBW

Army Form C. 2118

WAR DIARY
or
INTELLIGENCE SUMMARY
(Erase heading not required.)

Instructions regarding War Diaries and Intelligence Summaries are contained in F.S. Regs., Part II. and the Staff Manual respectively. Title Pages will be prepared in manuscript.

Place	Date	Hour	Summary of Events and Information	Remarks and references to Appendices
STEENVOORDE	9th		Batt's. Musketry, Manual Training continued. Batt's Boxing Competition held in afternoon. Lt. Suplit proceeded on leave to England.	H.Q.H. Cay.n
"	10th		Batt's Musketry, Manual Training continued. Company football matches played. 1st 13 orders approved on leave to England. A draft of 1 Regt. + 18 rank & file joined the Batt.	H.Q.M. Bayn
"	11th		Batt's Musketry. Orders received that the Battalion will join the 63rd Bde. 21st Division and will leave STEENVOORDE on 13th inst: Boxing Competition concluded.	H.Q.N.Coyn
"	12th		The Batt'n paraded at 10.30 A.M. for inspection by the G.O.C. 3rd Div'n (Major. Gen: J.A. HALDANE) who addressed the Batt's, bidding them farewell on their departure from the Division.	Regt.Coyn
STEENVOORDE to BAILLEUL	13th		The Batt'n paraded at 8.30 AM and marched to BAILLEUL (via EECKE, FLÈTRE and METEREN) where they went into billets in the town. Weather during march was wet with a high wind.	1st + 2nd Coy.n
BAILLEUL to ARMENTIERES	14th		The Batt'n paraded at 1.30 p.m. and marched to ARMENTIERES to join the 63rd Bde: 21st. Div. relieving the 12th WEST YORKS REGT. who are transferred to the 3rd Division. On arrival at ARMENTIERES about 4.30 p.m. the Batt'n went into billets in the Town.	H.Q. + 2 Coy.n
A RMENTIERES	15th		LT STEELE rejoined from machinegun course at WISQUES. 2nd BRANCH joined on firing opposition from the 12th LANCERS.	H.Q + 2.Coy.n
"	16th		C.O. + Coy. Commanders inspected the Trenches it is expected by the Battalion in the morning. Lieut. P.J. Murphy (R.A.M.C) rejoined from Leave. CAPT. BAZETT R.A.M.C. who was attached to the Batt: during LT MURPHY's absence left to rejoin the 8th Field AMBULANCE.	H.Q + 2 Coy.n

WAR DIARY or INTELLIGENCE SUMMARY

Army Form C. 2118

Place	Date	Hour	Summary of Events and Information	Remarks and references to Appendices
ARMENTIERES	17th		Trenches. The Batt'n paraded at 4.30 p.m. + took over Nos. 67, 68 and 69 (also LILLE POST) S.E. of ARMENTIERES with their fighting strength as follows. LILLE ROAD Trenches were occupied by Companies as follows:— "A" Coy 67, "B" Coy 68, "C" Coy. 69 (LILLE POST "D" COY.). The Batt'n relieved the 8th LINCOLNS. There were no casualties during the relief. The trenches were in a very wet condition. A fairly quiet night succeeded a wet afternoon. A quiet night was spent.	Hardships
"	18th		Lt. BRANCH proceeded on leave to ENGLAND. Our guns were very active during the morning. The enemy replied by shelling Bde. Hqrs. + the Town. A quiet day in the trenches. A good deal of work was done on parapets etc. One Casualty during the day, PTE HARDIMAN (10719) being wounded badly in the jaw + head. The early morning was frosty this day, damp cold + unpleasant. Lt. T.G. GIBSON HORNE joined the Batt'n on first appointment from the 28th Bn. of LONDON (ARTIST) RIFLES.	transept BSR Stuyp
"	19th		Frosty the early morning. The Divisional Commander (BRIG. GEN. H.W. GLOSTER) visited the Trenches about 10 a.m. Lt BODEN returned from leave + took over resumed the duties of Adjutant. Quiet day. One man killed (See Sharpe 75 Coy) The work in Trenches progresses + there is much to be done.	BSR Stuyp TSO Stuck
"	20th		Been morning. The Brigadier General of this Brigade (63rd) Brig. Gen. E.R. HILL visited the Trenches about 11 A.M. Our artillery shelled enemy front line trenches + reprisals occurred in the shape of Whizz Bangs. 3 Men of "A" Coy were wounded.	TSO Stuck

WAR DIARY or INTELLIGENCE SUMMARY

Army Form C. 2118

Place	Date	Hour	Summary of Events and Information	Remarks and references to Appendices
ARMENTIERS	21/11/15		Nothing of importance happened until about 11 a.m at which time 2/Lt ROBINSON (Brennan) & Sergt Brennan (Brennan Sergt) & 3 men were wounded & 1 man & the Regt Sgt Major of D Coy were killed by accidental explosion of a Grenade. The Bn was relieved by the 8th LINCOLNS the relief being completed by 7.45 p.m, no casualties during the relief. Bn in billets at Armentiers. Stalwyn parties amounting to 450 men from the Battalion.	TSP
	22/11/15		Bn in billets. Nothing special to report. Lt Septh returned from leave. 2/Lt W J WOOD joined the Battalion for duty.	TSP
	23/11/15		Bn in billets. The Div Commander Maj Gen Jacobs inspected the Battalion & addressed the officers & Sergts. His chief remarks were to the effect that we as a regular Battalion were to be an example to the new Army Bns serving in the same Brigade. 2/Lt F.J.R. SIMPSON, & LT A.H. WINN = SAMPSON 2/LT E. N. SPOFFORTH joined the Battalion for duty.	TSP
	24/11/15		Batt in Billets. Orders to form the men at Govt. NIEPPE. The 8th Lincolns in trenches. Relief completed by 7.30 pm, no casualties. A quiet night was spent but after rain at 9 pm it frogs & snowed before dawn.	TSP
	25/11/15		During the morning we casually received a draft of a man slightly himself through the Right foot. The Artillery in the trenches were active but we did not sustain any Artillery damage.	TSP
	26/11/15			

WAR DIARY or INTELLIGENCE SUMMARY

Army Form C. 2118

Place	Date	Hour	Summary of Events and Information	Remarks and references to Appendices
ARMENTIERS	27/1/15		Quiet cold night. Was spent by patrols though again they had very little to report. The Enemy shewed over in our trenches several times saying We are fed up" but all such ceased when we fired a few rounds at their trench. In the evening the vicinity of the Dump was shelled but apart from sniping fire + a nervousness there was harm was done. IDLE.	
	28/1/15		Another remarkably quiet night. Our M. Gunners discovered several Enemy working parties + fired on certain fixed spots. The day was apart quiet except for Artillery much, at about 9.30 a.m. the enemy shied some very good shaving at a Barn near LIFE POST, they apparently thought it to be an Artillery Observation Post. CHARD FARM + PIGOTS FARM came in for attention also but apart from destroying a lookout post no harm was done.	
	29/1/15		During the night the weather broke up & rain fell incessantly. The Trenches became very bad in regards wet. Both sides were very quiet. In the evening at about 6.30 pm the Bath were relieved by the 8th LINCOLNS. The Bn. went back to its billets at ARMENTIERS. During the whole time of 4 days only one casualty occurred & that not from the Enemy. IDLE.	
	30/1/15		Working Parties were sent out from all Companies by 8.30 a.m. Returning to billets at 3pm. There was nothing special happening. Some slight shelling of ARMENTIERS but	

WAR DIARY
or
INTELLIGENCE SUMMARY

Army Form C. 2118

Place	Date	Hour	Summary of Events and Information	Remarks and references to Appendices
ARMENTIÈRES	22		No change this week. 2/Lt BEAR from the 10th Hussars joins the Battalion having been granted a commission from the rank of Colonel.	

T. Bl[...]
Lieut Colonel

A/ Mines Rgr.
Dec 1915.
Vol. XVII

131/7957

Army Form C. 2118.

WAR DIARY
or
INTELLIGENCE SUMMARY.
(Erase heading not required.)

Instructions regarding War Diaries and Intelligence Summaries are contained in F. S. Regs., Part II. and the Staff Manual respectively. Title pages will be prepared in manuscript.

Place	Date	Hour	Summary of Events and Information	Remarks and references to Appendices
ARMENTIERS	1-12-15		Battalion in Billets. Baths at PONT NIEPPE under 21st Divisional arrangements which are very good, a clean change & ironing rooms available there.	T.D.L.
"	2-12-15		Battalion supplies working parties of 4.50 men for work on C.T.'s & Subsidiary line	T.D.L.
"	3-12-15		Battalion relieves the 8th LINCOLNS in Trenches. Relief complete by 8.30 p.m. No casualties.	T.D.L.
"	4-12-15		Very quiet day & night in the Trenches. Enemy seem of the "live & let live type" Capt H.A Hanley left B'n to take over duties as instructor at Corps School at BLENDESQUES near ST OMER. Casualties during day 1 wounded (L.Cpl FEIST.	T.D.L.
"	5-12-15		Our Artillery awakens that of the Enemy during the afternoon & he replies by WHIZZ-BANGS on our Front Trenches but did no physical damage. The trenches are very bad & wet owing to the rain after the frost & places they are collapsing. The earth being of clayey nature is subject to falls & makes any weather revetments we going in very.	T.D.L.

Army Form C. 2118

WAR DIARY
or
INTELLIGENCE SUMMARY
(Erase heading not required.)

Instructions regarding War Diaries and Intelligence Summaries are contained in F.S. Regs., Part II. and the Staff Manual respectively. Title Pages will be prepared in manuscript.

Place	Date	Hour	Summary of Events and Information	Remarks and references to Appendices
ARMENTIERS	6/12/15		A quiet day & wet. Trench water a bit troublesome in the afternoon. We had one casualty Pte Butcher of D Coy being killed. T.D.H.	
	7/12/15		A little shelling in the morning & some shooting from the Enemy to the effect that they were fed up. The Bn were relieved by the 8th Devons relief being complete without casualties by 8.30 pm T.D.H.	
	8/12/15		Bn in billets. Nothing of importance occurred. Lt. AVISON, 2Lt F.E. COOMBE 2LT V.D CHAPMAN joined the Battalion. LT. GOING proceeded on leave T.D.H.	
	9/12/15		Our Guns bombarded parts of Enemy lines & village in rear & they replied in ARMENTIERS wounding two men eg 63 Pte King T 1047, Pte Avenall 2.LT. PERKINS joined Bn. T.D.H.	
	10/12/15		The Bn found working parties but part were cancelled. There was nothing unusual happened. T.D.H.	
	11/12/15		Bn in billets. LT SAPTE took command of 'C' Coy. & 2LT Brand took over Transport T.D.H.	

Army Form C. 2118

WAR DIARY
or
INTELLIGENCE SUMMARY
(Erase heading not required.)

Instructions regarding War Diaries and Intelligence Summaries are contained in F.S. Regs., Part II. and the Staff Manual respectively. Title Pages will be prepared in manuscript.

Place	Date	Hour	Summary of Events and Information	Remarks and references to Appendices
ARMENTIERS	12/11/15		Divine Service for the Bn was held. Maj Gen H. JACOBS attending. 2LTS AUSTIN & C.J. COTTAM joined the Battalion.	TDSL
	13/11/15		The Battalion relieved the 2nd LINCOLNS commencing at 5 p.m. Stuff from the Enemy shells on Breen in Armentiers & killed Pte Bailey (10315). Wounding C/Sgt Stroyd Berkeley, Cpls ALLSWORTH, JENKINS, HARMAN, BRADLEY, BUCKLAND & LINKS. No casualties during relief.	TDSL
	14/11/15		A quiet day & nor was spent. We sustained a casualty by Sgt Goodge Mitchell being killed. (Sniper)	TDSL
	15/11/15		During the 15th we bombarded the trenches opposite no 69 & 70 Trenches preparing to an net cutting Bn's enterprise which was to take place early on the 16th. The Enemy trenches wire was well cut & our heavy Artillery which fires on the RAILWAY SALIENT did good shooting. During the day we sustained a casualty thro' fairly heavy shelling. 7424 Pte MITCHELL being killed.	TDSL

Place	Date	Hour	Summary of Events and Information	Remarks and references to Appendices
ARMENTIERS	16/12/15		The "Cutting Out" Enterprise which had been undertaken by the 8th Somerset Light Infantry who were on our left was due to start at 3.10 a.m. In perfect silence the 120 A, 6 O & men chosen for the duty & 3 Officers advanced at the Enemy Wire at 3.15 A.M, & entered the Enemy Trench at 3.17 A.M. without a single shot being fired at them. Our Barrage of fire was erected at 3.18 (to the second) on the Enemy C.T's. Our guns were most accurate & did excellent execution amongst the Enemy (the 139th Regiment, 11th Saxon Division, who had bolted on our entry to their trenches. The Enemy did not show much fight & those who remained were bayonetted or Bombed. Much information was gained from papers in the Signaleers Dug Out & the Coy Commanders. It was surprising to find that the advance of our men was quite unobserved by Enemy sentries even after the Wire cutting by our Guns during the day. The whole enterprise was carried out without a single casualty & the raiding party returned to their Trench within a mishap. The Trenches were then heavily shelled no 69 Trench especially & the raiders were caught by this fire & 3 killed & 7 wounded no 69 was held by our B Coy (Capt. Woolcombe) & for fully an hour a bombardment by Trench Mortars, 7.7 & other shells causing much	

WAR DIARY or INTELLIGENCE SUMMARY

Army Form C. 2118

Place	Date	Hour	Summary of Events and Information	Remarks and references to Appendices
ARMENTIERS	16/12/15	—	damage to Trenches but though the bombardment was an intense one losses were very light. Our front trenches for the whole day & night being 2 killed & 20 wounded. Amongst the latter was Captain Harris who was badly hit in the head by part of a Trench Mortar Bomb.	
	17/12/15		After 7 a.m. the Artillery on both sides was quiet, probably owing to the mist which prevented observation. Our casualties during day being 3 wounded, amongst who was 2Lt S.J. BEAR.	
	18/12/15		The day was uneventful & except for a few T.M's during the day nothing of an extraordinary nature happened. The scheme of relieving the number of troops in the front line trenches was commenced & one platoon of the Coy in t68 trench took over part of the Subsidiary line near CHAPELLE D' ARMENTIERS. Our casualties was 3 wounded.	
	19/12/15		An Enemy day of retaliation for at 6.30 A.M. the enemy exploded two mines which formed Craters about 30 feet diameter & about 20 feet deep but they were luckily arranged & were 30 yards short of the parapet of the MUSHROOM (Trench 70) held by the Somerset L.I. Our guns immediately opened fire & the enemy were unable to occupy the craters. The actual	

WAR DIARY
or
INTELLIGENCE SUMMARY
(Erase heading not required.)

Army Form C. 2118

Place	Date	Hour	Summary of Events and Information	Remarks and references to Appendices
ARMENTIERS	19/11/15		explosions caused no casualty but in subsequent bombardment of our line we sustained 1 Officer Killed & 9 wounded. The Officer 2Lt C.J. COTTAM who had only joined the Battalion on the 12th tho'gh mortally wounded was most devoted to his duties & his last words were of encouragement to his men, & said 'take charge of these other & keep a sharp look out in front.' He was buried at CHAPELLE D'ARMENTIERS. The Battalion were relieved at 8.30 p.m. by the 8th LINCOLNS & with the exception of 'C' Coy which remained in support at ARMENTIERS, to 'A' Coy returned to Billets at 3.p.m. The Battalion Billets at ARMENTIERS. 'D' Coy returned to Billets at TROU Battalion Quarters at PONT NIEPPE. TROU	
	20/11/15		On resting but some working Parties in all 450. Weather TROU	
	21/11/15		On resting. 2Lt STEELE proceeded on leave. nothing of note happened TROU	
	22/11/15		On relieved the 8th LINCOLNS in Trenches & relief complete without casualties by 8.30 p.m. The Enemy had made several futile attempts to reoccupy the craters formed by his mines in front of the MUSHROOM but in	

Army Form C. 2118

WAR DIARY
or
INTELLIGENCE SUMMARY

(Erase heading not required.)

Instructions regarding War Diaries and Intelligence Summaries are contained in F. S. Regs., Part II. and the Staff Manual respectively. Title Pages will be prepared in manuscript.

Place	Date	Hour	Summary of Events and Information	Remarks and references to Appendices
ARMENTIERS	23/12/15		Case they were fractious. They then resorted to stopping forward to run out their parallel saps from their trench. The Commanding Officer of the 8th Somerset Light Infantry LT COL. L. C. HOWARD was unfortunately reconnaissance at about 10.30 pm & was killed. In his person-and during the cutting out enterprise he had just been announced the Distinguished Service Order. TDSO	
	24/12/15		Very little activity on either side during the day, but at night the Germans rifle fire was very active. The Enemy were heard singing during the night & about 12 mn the Enemy fire quietened down. They were heard to shout "We Want Peace" we replied until 5 am rapid. Trumpeners of 50 H&O men from the Bn TDSO 25/12/15 Christmas Day, quiet resigned for about 2 hours after light & then the 23rd Divisional artillery fired five. The Enemy retaliated by shelling Chappelle D'ARMENTIERS. Our artillery fired a few rounds also. The Enemy in places made overtures probably to try & fix up an Unofficial Truce but not actually on our front. They did not get one. There were no Casualties (aSomme) during the day TDSO	
	26/12/15			

Army Form C. 2118

WAR DIARY
or
INTELLIGENCE SUMMARY
(Erase heading not required.)

Instructions regarding War Diaries and Intelligence Summaries are contained in F. S. Regs., Part II. and the Staff Manual respectively. Title Pages will be prepared in manuscript.

Place	Date	Hour	Summary of Events and Information	Remarks and references to Appendices
KEMMEL	26/12/15		A wet & misty day. Not much activity on either side. Casualties nil. TBOE	
	27/12/15		A bombardment of Enemy Trenches opposite the MUSHROOM commenced 12.45 pm & continued intermittently until 3 pm. The retaliation was very poor. Our Trench mortars very busy. The Bn. were relieved by the 8th LINCOLNS the relief being complete by 8.30 pm. TBOE Bn in billets. 400 men supplied to working Parties. TBOE	
	28/12/15		Bn. resting. The men Xmas Dinners & the issue of Gifts were not placed. The puddings sent from different sources were sufficient to supply each individual with a liberal helping. In the evening concerts were held by companies & a pleasant time was spent. TBOE	
	29/12/15		Bn. still found working parties. Nothing special happened. 2nd Lt WILLIS proceeds on leave.	
	30/12/15		Bn relieved the 8th Lincolns. Showers.	
	31/12/15		& rifle fire & via a lot of Shelling. This is via a lot of Shelling. At 11 pm the Enemy opened bursts of M.G. & rifle fire & via a lot of Shelling. This is to welcome the new year for their time is 1 hour previous to ours. Nothing special happened up till midnight. T/Boden Lt	H Pub&Lt T/Boden Lt

1875 Wt. W593/826 1,000,000 4/15 J.B.C. & A. A.D.S.S./Forms/C. 2118.

3

2ⁿᵈ Div
6/71
4th Middlesex Regt.
Jan
Vol. XVIII

21ˢᵗ Div

WAR DIARY or INTELLIGENCE SUMMARY

Army Form C. 2118

Place	Date	Hour	Summary of Events and Information	Remarks and references to Appendices
ARMENTIERS	1-1-16		The New Year was ushered in by the Germans at 11 pm according to our time, our course being 1 hour behind their time. They opened up a rifle fire with rifles & M. Guns & shouted but when they saw we not answering their shots were very high & no damage was done. At 1 am a Bombing but enterprise by the 23rd Div was carried out & as a result our trenches were very heavily shelled especially 67 & 68. The bombardment lasted for nearly two hours & Trench howitzers, 7.7 & grenades all fell in the section occupied by C & B Coys respectively. Our casualties were 5 killed & 30 wounded (5 slight). Towns shown everything seemed to resume its normal attitude & no further casualties occurred during the day. TD [sig]	
	2-1-16		The Enemy artillery were active during the morning & successfully located a Battery near CHAPELLE D'ARMENTIERS. The enemy brought up some heavy guns especially for this purpose. About 120 heavy 8" shells fell around the Battery, some very good shooting was done, but no direct hits occurred. Only one gun was damaged slightly & the guns were safely got out during the night. The casualties amongst the gunners were only one killed but some further. 4 R.E were caught in a cellar & 7 were killed. Capt T.S. WOOLCOMBE left the trenches for temporary duty with munition worker investigating 2nd Army. Our casualties were nil TD [sig]	

Army Form C. 2118

WAR DIARY
or
INTELLIGENCE SUMMARY
(Erase heading not required.)

Instructions regarding War Diaries and Intelligence Summaries are contained in F. S. Regs., Part II. and the Staff Manual respectively. Title Pages will be prepared in manuscript.

Place	Date	Hour	Summary of Events and Information	Remarks and references to Appendices
ARMENTIERS	3/1/16		Unusually quiet night, hardly a shot fired, probably due to the rain. No casualties. 2nd Lt. C. E. Going & Lieut. St. John Jones returned to Field Amb, the former suffering with shock. TDSR	
	4/1/16		Nothing to report, all quiet on front, Bn relieved by 8th LINCOLNS relief being complete at 8.20 pm TDSR	
	5/1/16		Bn in Billets. Usual working party of 400 provided. TDSR	
	6/1/16		Battn Bathed at Pont Muppe. Usual inspection on. Major H. P. J Bicknell assumes temporary rank of Lt Colonel vice Temporary Lt Col BRIDGMAN who relinquishes temporary rank TDSR	
	7/1/16		Working party of 400 found by Bn. Nothing to report TDSR	
	8/1/16		Bn relieves the 6th LINCOLNS in trenches, relief complete at 7.30 pm. No casualties TDSR	

Army Form C. 2118

WAR DIARY
or
INTELLIGENCE SUMMARY
(Erase heading not required.)

Instructions regarding War Diaries and Intelligence Summaries are contained in F.S. Regs., Part II. and the Staff Manual respectively. Title Pages will be prepared in manuscript.

Place	Date	Hour	Summary of Events and Information	Remarks and references to Appendices
ARMENTIERS	9/6		A quiet day & much work was done to improve the Trenches which in parts are in a very bad state owing to the continual wet & low-lying country. Our Snipers claimed three hits in W.E.2 MACQUART Cemetery, & lot of movement has been seen there of late. Lieut Willis & Lt A Sapte Bombing O/O Coy respectively & gassed no Temporary Captain Cavalier one slightly wounded.	TD/c
	10/6		A Bright & clear day though plenty of Aerial Activity, one of our aeroplanes was brought down about 2½ miles S.W. of W.E.2 MACQUART. He was flying at me low an altitude & an enemy anti aircraft battery scored a direct hit. The pilot attempted to descend in Spiral Volplane but his machine burst into flame & fell nose foremost to earth. A minor enterprise which was carried out by a Brigade to our left (Br Bn) at 11.30 pm was successful & about 20 Germans were killed & two taken prisoner of the 133rd Saxon Regt. (The information at when the opposing troops are confirmed the enemy movements which have been received from other sources). The Enemy Artillery replies to our Trenches, especially 69 but caused no casualties	TD/c
	11/6		A Misty cold day & very little activity on either side. Enemy T.C. from as usual a CHAPELLE D'ARMENTIERS. Sniping active in that area. One hit claimed by us. Enemy very merry mid rifles & m guns at night & by the number of very nervy (one wounded)	TD/c

WAR DIARY
or
INTELLIGENCE SUMMARY

(Erase heading not required.)

Army Form C. 2118

Place	Date	Hour	Summary of Events and Information	Remarks and references to Appendices
ARMENTIERES	12/7/16		A quiet day. Enemy shelled the Subsidiary Line & Trench 67. The Battalion were relieved by the 10TH YORK & LANCS who are in Bde (6 3rd) Bde. A change has been made whereby the sectors held by the left Bns of the Brigade are now to be held by the Rifle. Thus the machine gunners. Trenches 70, 71, 72, 73, are to be held by no 9 the 8th LINCOLNS & 67, 68 & 69 to be held by the 8th Somerset L. Infantry & 10th York & Lancs. The Bn while occupying this sector have done a great deal of work in improving & manning these Trenches & it is a matter of regret that we are not to reap the fruit of our work laborer. The Relief was complete at 9.15pm. No casualties were sustained during the day & relief. Bn in Billets. Working parties of 450 found by us. TBDU	
	13/7/16			
	14/7/16		B. Baths at TONT NIEPPE. Reconnoitering parties visited the new part of the line to be held. Their reports were not encouraging as to the condition of the Trenches, but we all of the opinion that they can be improved & will be habitable in a little time and way of the experience in Trench work this Battalion has. TBDU	

Army Form C. 2118

WAR DIARY
or
INTELLIGENCE SUMMARY

(Erase heading not required.)

Instructions regarding War Diaries and Intelligence Summaries are contained in F. S. Regs., Part II. and the Staff Manual respectively. Title Pages will be prepared in manuscript.

Place	Date	Hour	Summary of Events and Information	Remarks and references to Appendices
ARMENTIERES	15/1/16		Bn relieved the 8th LINCOLNS in the New Sector. The relief was completed by 8.45pm. Two Coys (A & B) occupy Trenches 71, 72 & 73, whilst D Coy holds the MUSHROOM & Trench 70. C. Coy is in support on the SUBSIDIARY LINE & are to relieve D Coy after 48 hours. No casualties. T.S.B.	
	16/1/16		The Trenches in this Sector are very wet & the line is most irregular. The Mushroom is a Salient & is a perfect Gruyere about a foot deep in places. The Communication Trenches are waterway now, they shelter any in the summer time. The parapet in several places, in fact in practically the whole of the line is not bullet proof & owing to recent activities is in a most wretched state. The Germans after a raid of the Somerset L. Infantry about the middle of December (which was unsuccessful) have continually bombed our French trenches & it is an abnormal extent & have worn them down on the line to quite a mark by the previous occupants. It must stand mp to gun an view of the active role to form in near page. During this day we increase 3 casualties from a Sniper who is very keen on a point between no 69 Trench & the entrance to the MUSHROOM. He has been located & is to receive attention tomorrow. T.S.B.	

Army Form C. 2118

WAR DIARY
or
INTELLIGENCE SUMMARY
(Erase heading not required.)

Instructions regarding War Diaries and Intelligence Summaries are contained in F. S. Regs., Part II. and the Staff Manual respectively. Title Pages will be prepared in manuscript.

Place	Date	Hour	Summary of Events and Information	Remarks and references to Appendices
ARMENTIERS	17/1/16		During the morning there was much Aerial Activity it being a clear morning & good for Observation. One of our machines flying very low was extremely fired at by rifle & machine guns but though punctured in no less than six places got a direct hit on the Enemy sniper who was spotter flash away. The part remained unhurt. The remainder of the day. We have already garrisoned an officer reconnoitring over the Enemy sniper. Our Casualties during the day were nil. TBE.	
	18/1/16		A bright day & much activity in both areas both Aerial & by Artillery. The Railway Sidings was much bombarded with apparently good results. Our Snipers claimed one hit. Our Casualties were 2 wounded. Lt Burbeck being his early in the morning by a stray bullet while in a Dugout. TBE.	
	19/1/16		A quiet day – nothing special to report. We were relieved by the 8th Lincolns at 6 p.m. No Casualties. It succeeded Smoke attack by Bayonet on left. TBE.	
	20/1/16		In billets at Armentieres. The usual Working party was found by the Bn. & Lieut Jackson proceeded on leave. TBE.	
	21/1/16		In billets in PONT NIEPPE BATHS. The usual inspection took place. TBE.	

WAR DIARY
or
INTELLIGENCE SUMMARY

Army Form C. 2118

Place	Date	Hour	Summary of Events and Information	Remarks and references to Appendices
ARMENTIÈRES	22/-/16		Working Parties again found by Battalion, Working opened & report.	TOE
-,,-	23/-/16		Church Parades for the Battalion. Relieved the 8th LINCOLNS in the Trenches at 8 p.m. No casualties during relief. Lieut LOFTS & 2.LT. WHITBY joined the Batt. for duty.	TOE
-,,-	24/-/16		Preparatory to a minor enterprise by the Durham Loyalists the Enemy wire was cut by the Artillery on each side of the Craters in front of the mushroom. The Enemy retaliated on the trench & seen of mushroom (Trench 70) & blew down the entrance to the mushroom called YORKSHIRE POST & the garrison which had been previously withdrawn from the mushroom were unable to reoccupy their original posts before and. During this bombardment our casualties were 2 killed & 9 wounded. The reports on the operation was cutting away, but some gaps were made. 2.LT. CHURCHFIELD joined the Batt.	TOE TOE
-,,-	25/-/16		During the night the Enemy reinforcements freely to our h. Some who were trying to repair the Enemy repairing the gaps in this wire, & were apparently in a state of nerves. He threw some trench mortars at our forward bombing posts. (Continues)	

WAR DIARY
or
INTELLIGENCE SUMMARY

Army Form C. 2118

Place	Date	Hour	Summary of Events and Information	Remarks and references to Appendices
ACHIET/ELAS	25/1/16		in the Sap but they fell short. The rain prevented by the O.C. Div Cyclists was known to commence at 9.95 pm from the Saps in front of the mushroom. The Grenadier parts in the Sap were unknown at 9.15 & the Cyclists took their places. The object of the raid which was known to last for twenty minutes, was to obtain as much information as to the identity of the Enemy & to obtain as many prisoners as possible. The orders were to be silence & the programme to be freely used. The Company (A) who were occupying the Mushroom & Trench 70 were to be prepared (& were) for any counter attack by the Enemy. The raiding party, about 34 strong including 5 officers of the Cyclists Bay, were in the Sap & a patrol was sent out to reconnoitre at 9.30p.m. & reported favourably. At 9.50 p.m the raiding company headed by a party of ten of the Cyclists & an officer at C.H. were in the Enemy in front of their wire. Two Coys of the Enemy were in the Offices & on the pstrol was encountered. The Cyclists continued to move forward & worked in front of the German wire were shot down by rifle fire. The remainder of the Cyclists then fallen for the Sap & much confusion was caused as the front	

Army Form C. 2118

WAR DIARY
or
INTELLIGENCE SUMMARY
(Erase heading not required.)

Place	Date	Hour	Summary of Events and Information	Remarks and references to Appendices
ARMENTIERS	25/7/16		when the Supts enter movement & forgot of the Mushroom. Their casualties were 2 Officers killed one officer wounded & 3 men killed & 7 men wounded. The lesson learned from this minor enterprise are I Reconnoitre properly. II Ensure that all patrolling know the ground & what is expected of them. Every man to know what to do if the enterprise fails. III Do not be too ambitious. IV The enterprise was a failure. In the subsequent bombardment which was chiefly carried out with Trench Mortars from the Enemy we lost 3 killed & 2 wounded. Amongst the former being Coy Sergt Major Marker.	
	26/7/16		During the morning at about 11.30 vicinity of Battalion Headquarters & "HAYSTACK FARM". A dug out at this later place was blown down & buried five of the Bn Grenadiers who had come off duty from the MUSHROOM during the early hours of the morning. Beaven thirty minutes the men but three were already dead. One succumbed to another dose of wounds. Of the other Grenadiers 8 received wounds or severe shock. Our total casualties during the day were 5 killed 13 wounded. MAJOR (Grntn)	

Army Form C. 2118

WAR DIARY
or
INTELLIGENCE SUMMARY

(Erase heading not required.)

Instructions regarding War Diaries and Intelligence Summaries are contained in F. S. Regs., Part II. and the Staff Manual respectively. Title Pages will be prepared in manuscript.

Place	Date	Hour	Summary of Events and Information	Remarks and references to Appendices
ARMENTIERS	26/1/16		Brown of the Bn Middlesex was attached to this Bn for two days instruction in the trenches. TJSL	
	27/1/16		During the early morning there was some naval activity & the Enemy shelling was heavy. The towns of ARMENTIERS & HOUPLINES were shelled. Our trenches also received attention. Our shelling replies & effectively silenced the Enemy. Casualties during the day were (one killed) (one wounded) The Bn were relieved at 6pm by the 8th LINCOLNS. TJSL	
	28/1/16		Bn in billets. The usual working partys were found. TJSL	
	29/1/16		Bn bathed at PONT NIEPPE. Nothing special to report. TJSL	
	30/1/16		Bn Church Parades during the morning. A rest day except for the usual inspections. TJSL	

Army Form C. 2118

WAR DIARY
or
INTELLIGENCE SUMMARY
(Erase heading not required.)

Place	Date	Hour	Summary of Events and Information	Remarks and references to Appendices
ARMENTIERS	31/1/16		Owing to a change in the plans of the Division with regard to the holding of the Trenches the Battalion will pursue to the Trenches until the night of 1st February. It has been so arranged that one Brigade will always be in Divisional Reserve. New Sectors of the Divisional front are therefore to be held by the Battalions & continual change of front will be entailed. The Trenches we are to hold are two 19, 75, 76, & part of 77. This portion of the line is on the left of our old position in front of HOUPLINES. T.R.D.Sr.	

Mitchell Lieut Colonel
Comndg 9th Bn
Middlesex Regt

WAR DIARY
or
INTELLIGENCE SUMMARY
(Erase heading not required.)

Army Form C. 2118

1. MUSHROOM
2. TRENCH 70
3. " 71
4. " 72 & part 73
5. TRENCH TRAMWAY
6. SUPPORTS
7. CRATERS OF GERMAN MINES
8. OUR SAPS
9. ENEMY SAPS NOW TRENCHES
9. YORKSHIRE POST
10. PETIT PORT EGAL FARM
11. ENTRANCE UNDER PARAPET TO SAP
12. WATERLOGGED C.Ts.

Army Form C. 2118

WAR DIARY
or
INTELLIGENCE SUMMARY
(Erase heading not required.)

Instructions regarding War Diaries and Intelligence Summaries are contained in F. S. Regs., Part II. and the Staff Manual respectively. Title Pages will be prepared in manuscript.

Place	Date	Hour	Summary of Events and Information	Remarks and references to Appendices
ARMENTIERS	1/2/16		Battalion relieves the 1st Bn LINCOLNS in the new front (low) of the line. Trenches 74, 75, 76 & part of 77 being held in the front line by D & C Coys. Support Trenches 74, 79 SS & Supplying Point X (S.P.X.) being held by A Coy & 75, 76, 77 being & S.T.Y. being held by B Coy. The relief was completed by 8.30 pm. One casualty being announced TBW	Trench Strength 693.
	2/2/16		A bright morning & the Enemy shelled our front line trenches with 7.7c. Street & St. Jacksen, Coy Sergt Major VAUSE & two others being wounded thereby. The new trenches are fairly firm but need a great deal of strengthening, they are however the largest trenches in this part of the line near Armentiers. TBW	
	3/2/16		The day was again bright & clear & there was much Aerial activity. The Artillery on both sides being busy. Except for a few 77s our Trenches were left alone. The Enemy Snipers were very inactive but at night his M. Guns fired continuously from about 6 pm until 9 pm, however very little of any great importance in the shooting. J.B.C. & A. A.D.S.S. getting working 9 rather pierdes TBW	

Army Form C. 2118

WAR DIARY
or
INTELLIGENCE SUMMARY
(Erase heading not required.)

Place	Date	Hour	Summary of Events and Information	Remarks and references to Appendices
ARMENTIERS	9/2/16		During the morning which was bright there was much shrapnel activity & some shells of about 9.7 calibre fell in the reserve trenches near No 79 point, there were no casualties. Orders were received during the day that a new system of relieving the front line was to be taken into practice the following night. This new scheme was that the frontage at present held by three Battalions of Brigade is to be held by two only, so as this only certain long with be held, thus giving a succession of strong posts. This means less men in the firing line & thus a greater immunity from shell fire. The necessity for trench & rival to be maintenance & the unremitting action of fire between posts is to be frequent patrolled & fires from or that the Enemy suspect no alteration in the system of holding the line. The front held by the Bn. is now about 1 mile. The new system is to be exception more impostor by the Comndng Officer & all Bn. Commanders during the day. T plans prepared for the several moves to take place next night. TBL The Enemy were again quiet during the day but having will be for at night. TBL There were no casualties during the day but any loss on Snipers claim a hit during the day. TBL	

Army Form C. 2118

WAR DIARY
or
INTELLIGENCE SUMMARY
(Erase heading not required.)

Instructions regarding War Diaries and Intelligence Summaries are contained in F.S. Regs., Part II. and the Staff Manual respectively. Title Pages will be prepared in manuscript.

Place	Date	Hour	Summary of Events and Information	Remarks and references to Appendices
ARMENTIERS	5/2/16		Enemy Snipers were busy all day & also one man in Evenness, several machine gunners between when taking pans, if anything our machine guns the evening. The Enemy apparently opened one of our supposing – Strong trench caters S.7.X.T. at about 4.30 p.m. Then heavy shells fell near this place they were 5".9" or as they are better known to the troops "Coal boxes" these were doing damage except turning up the earth. Company sent over the new portion of the line at 5.30 p.m. Casualties from shell fire during the day were 3 wounded. TBL	
	6/2/16		Enemy again shelled vicinity of supports. On the whole the day was quiet & our casualties were 1 wounded by Sniper & 1 S/Sergt Robinson accidentally killed by a M.Gunner. TBL	
	7/2/16		Quiet day, but wet. The Battalion was relieved by the 10th YORKSHIRE Regt of the 62nd Bde. The whole of the 63rd Bde were relieved this night & we moved to new billets in ARMENTIERS. The relief was complete by 9 pm. No casualties. TBL	

WAR DIARY
or
INTELLIGENCE SUMMARY
(Erase heading not required.)

Army Form C. 2118

Place	Date	Hour	Summary of Events and Information	Remarks and references to Appendices
ARMENTIERS	8/2/16		Battalion in billets. Working party was found daily by the Battalion.	
"	9th 10th 11th 12th		From the 8th to the 13th inst. Bn remained in billets in Armentiers. Two casualties occurred during this period whilst on working parties & two whilst in ARMENTIERS Town. One of whom subsequently died. TBDL	
	13/2/16		Bn moved to HOUPLINES & billeted in the village & in a factory known as the TISSAGE. Whilst riding over stones in the afternoon the Regtl Sgt Major was wounded & three men slightly wounded. Took over billets from the 10th K.O.Y.L.I. relief completed by 8.30 pm TBDL	

WAR DIARY
or
INTELLIGENCE SUMMARY

Army Form C. 2118

Place	Date	Hour	Summary of Events and Information	Remarks and references to Appendices
ARMENTIERS	14/2/16		Working party were found by the Battalion. HOUPLINES was shelled. No casualties. Major E.F.F. SANDYS joined the Bn. for duty & took over duties as 2nd in Command.	
	15/2/16		Quiet day & in the evening a few shells 7.7 fell near billets but no damage was done.	
	16/2/16		Bn. moved to billets & dug out near front of pres SUBSIDARY LINE NE of HOUPLINES. The Bn. is to remain in Support for three days before moving into the front Trenches. The men sleep out in the Subsidiary Line are billeted at a Brewery near the LOCK GATES. No casualties occurred during the day.	
	17/2/16		During the afternoon the Enemy shelled the vicinity of the new Bn. Hqrs with 5.9. No damage was done & no casualties occurred. Bn. Hqrs are at an old chateau in the hands of the LYS called CHATEAU LE ROSE. The Commany Officers of the Bn. in Command made the new forward fire line while we are in to relieve from	

Army Form C. 2118

WAR DIARY
or
INTELLIGENCE SUMMARY
(Erase heading not required.)

Instructions regarding War Diaries and Intelligence Summaries are contained in F.S. Regs., Part II. and the Staff Manual respectively. Title Pages will be prepared in manuscript.

Place	Date	Hour	Summary of Events and Information	Remarks and references to Appendices
ARMENTIERES	18/2/16		During these two days there is nothing special to report. Our Artillery carried out several bombardments but enemy retaliation was practically nil. No casualties.	
	19/2/16			
	20/2/16		At 5 am the Bn moved up into the front Trenches relieving men from the 10th YORK & LANCS the relief was complete at 7 am & Bn Hqrs moved to LOCK CHATEAU. The Trenches held are from 73 to 79 inclusive the left Trench (79) resting on the banks of the river near the village of FRELINGHEIN which is occupied by the Enemy. The Trenches are very wet & in a very bad condition owing to neglect & also in a measure due to the continuous	

Army Form C. 2118

WAR DIARY
or
INTELLIGENCE SUMMARY
(Erase heading not required.)

Place	Date	Hour	Summary of Events and Information	Remarks and references to Appendices
ARMENTIERES	29/2/16		continued rise & fall of the LYS which inundates the country around after rain. Our casualties during the day were 1 wounded. The Divisional Commander visited the Trenches during the morning	
	1/3/16		Our front was very quiet during the day. The Enemy artillery were out for long range shooting & shelled the vicinity of LE BIZET & caused some casualties amongst a battery near there. Our casualties during the day were two wounded.	
	2/3/16		The early morning was very quiet & the Trenches were in fair [?] just prior to [?]. The Brigade during the day to the effect that the 25th Divisional Commander wished all ranks to put in as much work as possible to improve the Trenches we now occupy so that the next Division relieving us would not be able to complain of the state of the Trenches. Troops agreed [?] we were sent up to [?] working parties from the Reserve Battalion at Le TISSAGE & BRASSERIE worked [?] might be much more were put out at night to go to the cavalry now improving. Our Casualties during the day were 1 Dead & 1 wounded & 1 Woman.	[signatures]

Army Form C. 2118

WAR DIARY
or
INTELLIGENCE SUMMARY
(Erase heading not required.)

Place	Date	Hour	Summary of Events and Information	Remarks and references to Appendices
ARMENTIERS	23/2/16		During the morning a Bombardment of the Enemy Trenches opposite Trenty 2 was carried out prior to an enterprise which was being arranged by the 10th YORKSHIRE Regt. The Bombmt was not a enterprise. The shelling cut no wire although during the day & afternoon is considered to be successful. At 10.57 pm the artillery opened fire & at 11 pm raiser their elevation to barrage on the enemy communication & at the same time the cutting out party left their trenches and got to the German Wire. The party was composed of 50 Other ranks & 5 Officers. On arrival at the Enemy wire they were met by bombs, the enemy were waiting for them & have to retire. Their total casualties were about 15 wounded amongst whom was no Officer. It would appear that the Enemy was getting quite used to these enterprises & warned them at the gaps made in wire with Grenadier squads. The Enemy artillery retaliation was very poor & chiefly composed of 7.7s + Trench Mortars. We suffered no casualties from retaliation. (One man was wounded during the whole day). Col Bucknall proceeded to Staffane Very cold day. Major SANDYS is in Command whilst Col Bucknell is on leave. During the many rumour from Bruges that prior to handing over to the 25th Division who are relieving us, the general emission of Trenches is to be improved & special attention paid to the wire. The latter part of the message has been	
	29/2/16			

Army Form C. 2118

WAR DIARY
or
INTELLIGENCE SUMMARY
(Erase heading not required.)

Place	Date	Hour	Summary of Events and Information	Remarks and references to Appendices
ARMENTIERS	25/2/16		Complete until 10.30pm. No Casualties. T.S.Oldacre Capt.	
	26/2/16		One killed in ARMENTIERS the billets occupied by Battalion being in the HOSPICE CIVIL. Working Parties were found by the Battalion in the evening. No Casualties T.S.Oldacre Capt.	
	27/2/16		Working Parties found by the Battalion as total of 500 being recruit. 2 LIEUT. E.T. WILLIAMS who was in charge from being wounded. During the afternoon the Co.O. & Staff visited the ARMENTIER DEFENCE LINES at BOIS GRENIER, LAVESEE, CHAPELLE D'ARMENTIERS, CHAPELLE ROMPUE, LA BIZET, LYS near HOUPLINES. Under the new system of the banks of the river LYS near HOUPLINES. Under the new system of holding the firing line one battalion is in Brigade reserve & one Brigade is in Divisional reserve. Therefore it may be necessary to move to either of these places in event of a successful enemy attack. There are gun positions built at these places except on the CHAPELLE D'ARMENTIER ROAD but there is a good deal there which is daily in very fair covert each seen to put in a state of defense. The enemy winning is also great. The bridge over the LYS has minus & sherries approaches during the wet months when the enemy means is inundated would form a formidable obstacle. Draft orders are to be made out for mines to	

1875 Wt. W593/826 1,000,000 4/15 J.B.C. & A. A.D.S.S./Forms/C. 2118.

WAR DIARY or INTELLIGENCE SUMMARY

Army Form C. 2118

Place	Date	Hour	Summary of Events and Information	Remarks and references to Appendices
ARMENTIERES	24/2/16		Attention to & much wire put out. The Trenches themselves have been greatly improved but much remains to be done. The left portion of our sector is extremely bad owing to its proximity to the L.T.5. However there is marked improvement already which fair weather gratifying. Work has been very much hampered by the hard frost & snow. Our patrols have worn white clothing for night patrolling & find it very effective the Enemy trine it not the rifle fire man during the day & found it more effective. Our snipers claimed no less & one gunny. We had no casualties during the day but one man was hit theour failure. It was of Gnr. Tay. & 5th green th. Batt. -S.Beard	
	25/2/16		The O.C. are to be relieved by the 10th YORKSHIRE Regt tonight. In summing up total amount of work done the following interesting totals are arrived at. 32 Knife rests put out, 69 coils of wire staked out & existing Knife rests moved further out from our parapet. There are now few points in the line to allow any of the Enemy to throw a trench into the Trench. 50 Trench Boards have been raised & old ones raised & cleared of mud & water. Each bay has now a number boared with hoof Trench & No of Bay painted on it, the work of our Sirman. The evening was very bad for the relief as it was Snowing very hard & the Trenches were very slippery. The relief therefore was not	

Army Form C. 2118

WAR DIARY
or
INTELLIGENCE SUMMARY
(Erase heading not required.)

Place	Date	Hour	Summary of Events and Information	Remarks and references to Appendices
REMEMBER	27/5/16		either of their phones. This was done during the evening by Major Sandys. At about 11:30pm two Bells were heard ringing in a northerly direction—all day officers immediately from their Corps & were about to turn out when a message from Bryant told us that the whole alarm was the result of an accident. It, however, proved that the chain of sound was good. T.B.Capt.	
	28/5/16		During the morning the Bn were on fatigue under the R.E. there being much still to be done on Defences. No casualties. T.B.Capt.	
	29/5/16		The Bn are in reserve today. The orders on each day as that all we to be ready to turn out at a moment's notice. Inspection of Arms & Equipment were carried out during the day & men had a real & chance to clean up their kits etc. T.B.Capt. (Later) Orders saying that the move of the Division to rest are cancelled for the time being. T.B.Capt.	

Fishall
Lt.Col. Commdg 9th Middlesex

Instructions regarding War Diaries and Intelligence Summaries are contained in F. S. Regs., Part II. and the Staff Manual respectively. Title Pages will be prepared in manuscript.

WAR DIARY
or
INTELLIGENCE SUMMARY

(Erase heading not required.)

Army Form C. 2118

Place	Date	Hour	Summary of Events and Information	Remarks and references to Appendices

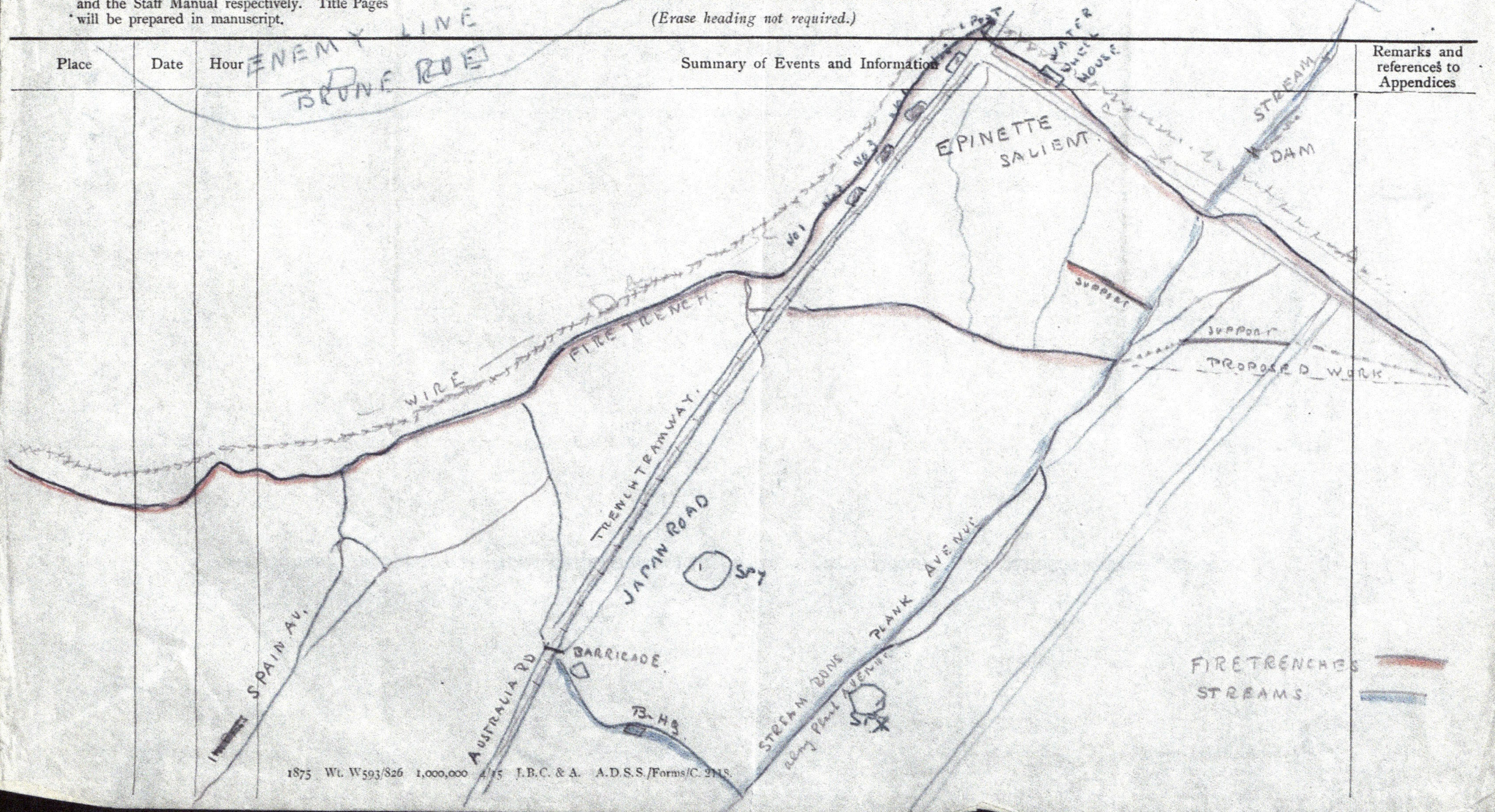

ENEMY LINE
EPINETTE
SALIENT
STREAM
DAM
SUPPORT
SUPPORT
PROPOSED WORK
FIRE TRENCH
WIRE
No 1
No 2
No 3
TRENCH TRAMWAY
JAPAN ROAD
SP7
BARRICADE
AUSTRALIA RD
B. HQ
SPAIN AV.
PLANK AVENUE
FIRETRENCHES
STREAMS

1875 Wt. W593/826 1,000,000 4/15 J.B.C. & A. A.D.S.S./Forms/C. 2118.

63 5/21

4 Middlesex Regt

Vol XX

Army Form C. 2118

WAR DIARY
or
INTELLIGENCE SUMMARY
(Erase heading not required.)

Instructions regarding War Diaries and Intelligence Summaries are contained in F.S. Regs., Part II. and the Staff Manual respectively. Title Pages will be prepared in manuscript.

Place	Date	Hour	Summary of Events and Information	Remarks and references to Appendices
ARMENTIERS	1/3/16		The Bn furnish working parties of 5.30 in separate parties morning & evening & two Coys bathed in the morning at PONT NIEPPE baths. One man was wounded whilst with a working party. Operation Orders were received that the Bn move to the trenches in ETINETTE SALIENT tomorrow night. The Bn has been in these trenches before. B.O. + Coy visited new line which is rather wet & unparapetted.TBBCapt.	
	2/5/16		Remainder of Bn bathed during the morning. In the evening the relief commenced at 6.pm. being completed by 9.pm. The trenches held are 72 – 77. We relieved the 9rd Bn K.O.Y.L.I. Disposition of Bn are as follows. A Coy. 72 & 73. Trenches (Right Coy) C. Coy 79 & 75 Trenches (Centre Coy) D Coy 76 & 77 Trenches (Left Coy) B Coy in reserve in trench SS 75 & 76. There were no casualties during relief. — See attached map of trenches — TSBCapt.	
	3/5/16		A quiet morning & not very clear. The Artillery bombarden the Enemy Trenches opposite the MUSHROOM at 12.0 . They retaliated at about 2.15 p.m on our 70, 71, 72, 73, 74 Trenches which their artillery enfilaves from	

Army Form C. 2118

WAR DIARY
or
INTELLIGENCE SUMMARY
(Erase heading not required.)

Instructions regarding War Diaries and Intelligence Summaries are contained in F. S. Regs., Part II. and the Staff Manual respectively. Title Pages will be prepared in manuscript.

Place	Date	Hour	Summary of Events and Information	Remarks and references to Appendices
ARMENTIERS	3/5/16		direction of FUNQUEREAU. Owing to our line being held very thinly & the intensive shelling by the enemy our casualties were nil, but it was rather unhappy for about an hour. 7.7 & 9.2 were the chief calibre shell used & small Trench mortars called by the troops "Sausages". Our snipers report one hit. TBDept. Col. Bicknell rejoined from leave	
	4/5/16		During the night Sleet fell increasingly & also during the morning until 12 noon. The situation therefrom have assumed the semblance of mill streams & flooded many Trenches & Dugouts. The Enemy were very quiet during any day but at about 5 pm he commenced with some field guns & we retaliated; no damage was done. The work on the Trenches is greatly handicapped by the weather. The Trenches are feeling in where they are unrevetted & Bn Hqrs on PLANK AVENUE is partially flooded out. Working Parties from Reserve Battalion have been applied for to expedite the work which is accumulating. Gun Corselli during the day were hit. TBDept	The Divisional General Jacobs was wounded & G.S.O.I Col DANIELS killed in billets in ARMENTIERS
	5/5/16		During the night it was freezing & extra fuel was sent up for the firing line Enemy Hqrs were busy from about 8 pm till 10 pm. It was proposed by the R.E. that a dam be placed across a stream which every flows from	

WAR DIARY
or
INTELLIGENCE SUMMARY
(Erase heading not required.)

Army Form C. 2118

Place	Date	Hour	Summary of Events and Information	Remarks and references to Appendices
ARMENTIERS	5/3/16		Enemy tried across 'No Mans Land' across Trench 73 & down PLANK AVENUE. The object aimed at being to show the bravest of the stream to flood the Enemy Trenches. This was done by 'C' Coy under the command of LT FRY. A certain amount of success was attained but the results to the enemy Trenches were not found out. The level of the stream in the Enemy area of stream was raised quite 3 feet. In answer to a memo from the Bde. lists of names of Officers, NCOs & men were sent in for recommendation to names for continuous good work in the Trenches. The names will be found in the margin. Our casualties during day were Nil. T/Sept	For lettering shown. Capt Wollscroft. Capt BODEN. D.C.M. Sgt WALKER. " HORNER " WOOTTS Cpl TANDY LSgt BOWIE.
	6/3/16		Weather continues somewhat unpleasant trying & water began to fall lower. The Enemy was fairly quiet except for long range machine gun. Our casualties were nil. 1 Officer of the 8th Somerset L. Inf who was to relieve us arrived in the Trenches. T/Sept	
	7/3/16		We are to be relieved tonight by the 8th Somerset. During our time in the Trenches much work has been done chiefly in shortening army lines & strengthening army points. Much wire has been put out about 83 coils & 200 stakes have been used. The day	

WAR DIARY
or
INTELLIGENCE SUMMARY

Army Form C. 2118

Place	Date	Hour	Summary of Events and Information	Remarks and references to Appendices
ARMENTIERS	7/8/16		...cause of trouble in construction of new work is the amount of labour & quantity of material required in packing up caving parts which in many cases are entirely unreliable & in consequence the weather has caused wholesale collapses of parts. The weather which is at present continually pouring in in a great extent is in progress. However there is a great improvement in the condition of the line, no impression is to be got over. Our casualties during the day were 1 OR wounded.	
	8/8/16		A guide say had gone to the reservoir. The wounded has now and invariably must have been done on the river in front & also enemy snipping found. Called SPY & SPT. We were relieved by the 8th SOMERSET L.I. the relief being complete by 9.30 pm. Our casualties during the day were 1 Killed, 1 OR wounded.	T.B.Scott
	night 8/9 9/10 10/11 11/8/16		The Battalion were in ARMENTIERS, in Brigade Reserve. During these three days we found working parties of 150 per day. 4 reinfts of 2 Sergts & 43 men joined the Bn, most of them has been out before & had either been sick or wounded. During this period a new scheme of relieving the line was framed in order to simplify matters in trenching over to the 17th who relieved the 23rd next (continues) T.B.Scott	

WAR DIARY
or
INTELLIGENCE SUMMARY
(Erase heading not required.)

Army Form C. 2118

Place	Date	Hour	Summary of Events and Information	Remarks and references to Appendices
ARMENTIERES	11/3/15		(Continued) The men sent to Trenches 67, 68, 69, is to be taken in by the Bn. after those coy's in the Subsidiary line lost is to be held by two Coys in the firing line & 2 in Subsidiary LINE & LILLE POST. The Bn relieves the 2R LINCOLNS in the Subsidiary Line from LILLE ROAD to FARM DE LA BUTERNE, S.P. X, S.P. Y, & PORT EGAL REDOUBT, the relief being complete by 9.15 pm. T.S.D. Capt	
	12/3/15		Under this old system of trenches, the line the Bn in Subsidiary line (which is of course the Bn in support) occupies has a split-up & cover such a length of frontage that it wants to a sufficient extent to engage in certain circumstances & much work there is to left to the Coy commanders themselves. The work to be done is chiefly that requisite in the front line by the Bn there & parties are received daily to each Bn. Wiring is also being done in front practice by A Coy who lies to right of the line near the LILLE ROAD. The Enemy shelled the vicinity of CHAPELLE D'ARMENTIERES & were intermittently near Bn Hqrs near Sy FARM during the morning. The night was uneventful (with exception of none of Gunners). T.S.D. Capt	

WAR DIARY
or
INTELLIGENCE SUMMARY
(Erase heading not required.)

Army Form C. 2118

Place	Date	Hour	Summary of Events and Information	Remarks and references to Appendices
ARMENTIERES	13/3/16		The weather has suddenly decided to be spring like & the effect on the landscape is wonderful. The Trenches are getting drier & the probability of starting a drainage scheme to cope with wet winter water is being examined shortly. The Enemy Artillery were fairly active & again shelled the vicinity of CHAPELLE D'ARMENTIERS. We ourselves on Casualty during day (Wounded.)	T.B.Capt
	14/3/16		During the day working parties to the front Trenches were found by us & commencing at 7pm we relieved the 10th YORK & LANCS in Trenches 67, 68, 69 & LILLE POST. This found up in held by 2 Coys (B+C) in front line 80 men & 2 Officers of A Coy in LILLE POST remainder of A Coy in Rgte of Subsidiary line near LILLE ROAD while D Coy Hdrs left again & the Subsidiary line. The Bn on our Right was the Tyneside Scottish & on our left the 8 K LINCOLNS. The relief was complete about 9 pm. The Enemy were fairly active mid to Evens at night but we sustained no casualties.	T.B.Capt
	15/3/16		Except for shelling of CHAPELLE D'ARMENTIERS & Battery searching the Enemy were fairly quiet on our front. This afternoon were fairly active but no apparently replies. It was a splendid day for observing & ___ two Enemy Aeroplanes were busy over our lines. Ours were active to about eight of their Planes over in vicinity of LILLE at about 8 a.m. It is always noticeable that on fine days rider dart themselves to try. (over) J.B.	

1875 Wt. W593/826 1,000,000 4/15 J.B.C. & A. A.D.S.S./Forms/C. 2118.

WAR DIARY
or
INTELLIGENCE SUMMARY

Army Form C. 2118

Place	Date	Hour	Summary of Events and Information	Remarks and references to Appendices
ARMENTIERS	15/3/16		(continued) range artillery duels & Trenches mortars. He about eighty for Sergt Horsell was killed & Capt T.S Wolscombe & one man wounded. Major Sandy's revival given to proceed to England to take command.	
	16/3/16		Except for a little rifle and artillery shelling very little happened. No casualties. Capt D.C.T ROWLEY & 2LT C.A. ST JOHN JONES joined the Battalion.	T.O.Capt T.O.Capt
	17/3/16		During the morning the Corps Commander Gen Sir Charles FERGUSSON inspected the Trenches. The condition of the Strong points was not quite to his satisfaction but he saw that great progress had been made. He was accompanied by Brigadier General E.R. Hill. We had no casualties during the day. 2LTs. A.S. HAWKE & A.S. WILKINSON Officers of the 7th LINCOLN Regt who belong to the 17th Division which is to relieve us on the night of the 19/20th received the Trenches to reconnoitre & to get an idea of the work in hand. No casualties. 2LT E PEYTON joined Bn.	T.O.Capt T.O.Capt
	18/3/16			
	19/3/16		The Symetters of the relieving units The LEWIS detachment, & Grenadiers arrived at about 10 am to look over their respective posts & position of the line. The Enemy were very quiet & though a high day it was not good for observation. The relief was carried out thoroughly &	

Army Form C. 2118

WAR DIARY
or
INTELLIGENCE SUMMARY
(Erase heading not required.)

Instructions regarding War Diaries and Intelligence Summaries are contained in F. S. Regs., Part II. and the Staff Manual respectively. Title Pages will be prepared in manuscript.

Place	Date	Hour	Summary of Events and Information	Remarks and references to Appendices
ARMENTIERES	19/5/16		all information gathered during an reconnoitering yple seen haveur over on paper. The lift was complete by 9.30 p.m. The Division moving to billets in ARMENTIERS. There were no casualties during day. T.B.Sept	
	20/5/16		Division bathed in morning at PONT NIEPPE BATHS. Remainder of day spent in cleaning up & packing for the move to rest at STRAZEELE area. T.B.Sept	

	21/5/16		The Bn present ready to move off at 8 a.m. moving off in column of half coys at 200 yds interval. The route was via PONT NIEPPE, NIEPPE, STEENVERKE to LA CRECHE area where the night was to be spent. It is interesting to sum up the casualties of the Bn. whilst in the ARMENTIER Sector since Nov. 16th 1915 to present date. They are as follows:
			
			     Killed Wounded Total casualties
			Officers 1 7 8
			Other Ranks 32 140 172
			              Total 180
			
			For the period spent here this casualty list is not so heavy as in other units. T.B.	

Army Form C. 2118

WAR DIARY
or
INTELLIGENCE SUMMARY
(Erase heading not required.)

Instructions regarding War Diaries and Intelligence Summaries are contained in F.S. Regs., Part II. and the Staff Manual respectively. Title Pages will be prepared in manuscript.

Place	Date	Hour	Summary of Events and Information	Remarks and references to Appendices
STRAZEELE	21/3/16		Parts of the time held by the Battalion.	
	22/3/16		The Bn arrived at billets in LA CRECHE area at about midday after a very trying march to the Bn although the distance was only about 8 miles the men felt it badly after their spell of Trench work which does not allow of much exercise in route marching. T.B.Capt.	
			Bn moved off from billets to the remainder of journey to STRAZEELE at 10 am. The weather was damp & slightly raining. The route was via OUTTERSTEENE, MERIS, STRAZEELE. The Battalion arrived at about 2 pm & that same their respective billets. The Bn area is very scattered but is of fair weather premises, otherwise to quite some & afford plenty of room for training. T.B.Capt.	
	23/3/16		Companies of work under arrangements & orders of Coys. Rain however prevented work being done. T.B.Capt. LT AVISON rejoined Bn.	
	24/3/16		The rain & sleet which fell during the night prevented Coys doing much work but time drew not there were but seemed to recover to return to their W.A. DDLING games Bn as Bn in Billets. T.B.Capt	

Army Form C. 2118

WAR DIARY
or
INTELLIGENCE SUMMARY
(Erase heading not required.)

Instructions regarding War Diaries and Intelligence Summaries are contained in F.S. Regs., Part II. and the Staff Manual respectively. Title Pages will be prepared in manuscript.

Place	Date	Hour	Summary of Events and Information	Remarks and references to Appendices
STRAZEELE	25/5/16		Coys carried out as men as possible their programme of work but the conversion of pioneers to the wet again prevented work. TDBayr	
	26/5/16		Church Services were cancelled owing to rain & recent Capt T.S. Workman rejoined Bn. TDBayt	
	27/5/16		A little outdoor work was done. Rain. LT STEELE joined Battalion. TDBayr	
	28/5/16		The Bn. went for a Route March to MONT-DE-CATS & Brigadier Gen E.R. HILL Commg 63rd Inf. Bde inspected Transport. Improvement in recent TDBayr. Sr Shrupe(MG) & 2Lieut. Brewer proceeded on leave TBB.	
	29/5/16		Bn. Route March, two Bn. marches have to be done during this rest period about 75% of the B. have been re-inoculated against enteric & during the preceding three days therefrom many have been quite unable to carry out the original training programme. Orders were received during the day that this [signed] to join the 13th Bde. TDBayr.	

Army Form C. 2118

WAR DIARY
or
INTELLIGENCE SUMMARY
(Erase heading not required.)

Instructions regarding War Diaries and Intelligence Summaries are contained in F. S. Regs., Part II. and the Staff Manual respectively. Title Pages will be prepared in manuscript.

Place	Date	Hour	Summary of Events and Information	Remarks and references to Appendices
STRAZEELE	30/5/16		Training was carried out by Coys in the morning & afternoon under several football matches were played amongst Coys & one Officers v Sergts the latter winning 3-0. The weather has improved wonderfully. The Bn is to entrain at 7.53 pm on the night of the 31st. TBBeasley	
	31/5/16		The Bn was spent chiefly in packing up for the journey to the new area. Kits were reduced to a minimum. at 7.20 pm the Bn marched to the station in one train at 7.40 pm. The division have spent & moved out of the station in one train at 7.40 pm. The division have spent in this area has not allowed of much other than sport & the weather has been fine, as there are not many reports at moving to a new area. Relieved & J R Simpson went on leave. TBBeasley	

JRickard Lt Col

3/21

4 Middlesex Regt

Vol XIX

63 Bdg

Army Form C. 2118

WAR DIARY
or
INTELLIGENCE SUMMARY
(Erase heading not required.)

Instructions regarding War Diaries and Intelligence Summaries are contained in F. S. Regs., Part II. and the Staff Manual respectively. Title Pages will be prepared in manuscript.

Place	Date	Hour	Summary of Events and Information	Remarks and references to Appendices
AMIENS	1/7/16		The train conveying the battalion from the outskirts of AMIENS to ALLONVILLE about 7 miles. We arrived at our billets at about 11.30 a.m. 12 miles from the firing line & is a clean healthy little place although difficulty may be experienced in procuring drinking water owing to enteric fever. During the remainder of the day the battalion rested. T.B.Booth	
			Church Service was held on the slopes of a small hill just above the village at 10:30 a.m. The remainder of the day was spent chiefly in cleaning of Equipment and resting. T.B.Booth	
ALLONVILLE	2/7/16		The Battalion arrived at LONGPRE about 7 a.m where we detrained. The march was hot & sunny into the town. The village of ALLONVILLE is about	
	3/7/16		The Battalion paraded for Drill under the Company Officers from 9.30 a.m till noon. In the evening the Battalion played Football against the R.F.C. and obtained a win of 2-0. The second Battalion "Fleming for" Officers passed through the village of QUERRIEU on the way to trenches near ALBERT. The Company Officers several other Officers & 60 men of the Drums of the Bn. met them at this village to see them pass, the Drums playing them through the village. T.B.Booth	

Army Form C. 2118

WAR DIARY
or
INTELLIGENCE SUMMARY
(Erase heading not required.)

Instructions regarding War Diaries and Intelligence Summaries are contained in F. S. Regs., Part II. and the Staff Manual respectively. Title Pages will be prepared in manuscript.

Place	Date	Hour	Summary of Events and Information	Remarks and references to Appendices
ALLONVILLE near AMIENS	4/4/16		Coys were at disposal of Coy Commanders who carried out advances formation etc. The Sergts of the Bn played the NCOs of the Royal Flying Corps at football during the game game 2-0. Sports & especially football is being played as much as possible by all ranks. The weather is very bright & sunny & the men are beginning to look fit for work again. TBB Capt.	
"	5/4/16		Coys at disposal of Coy Commanders. Nothing special to report. TBB Capt.	VIII
"	6/4/16		The Dummy Officer took over command of the Brigade during the absence on leave of Brig General E. R. Hill. Major W.A. Oakley resumed command of the Battalion. Coys were at disposal of Coy Commanders. Orders were received for move tomorrow the trenches. The Bn are to move to VILLE tomorrow near ALBERT men which place the new sector of line is to be held by the battalion is situated. TBB Capt.	

Army Form C. 2118

WAR DIARY
or
INTELLIGENCE SUMMARY
(Erase heading not required.)

Instructions regarding War Diaries and Intelligence Summaries are contained in F. S. Regs., Part II. and the Staff Manual respectively. Title Pages will be prepared in manuscript.

Place	Date	Hour	Summary of Events and Information	Remarks and references to Appendices
ALLONVILLE	7/5/16		The Bn moved off at 8 am from ALLONVILLE to march to VILLE a distance of about 12 miles. The day was good for marching & very few fell out en-route. Some difficulty was experienced at VILLE to find accommodation for all Coys & eventually D Coy & part of "C" were billeted in a village named BUIRE about a mile away. The rest of the Battalion was here, two greatly improved the harsh Discipline of the Battalion. We were settled down in our billets at about 5 pm. TBBoyr	
VILLE	8/5/16		A working party of 400 men from among the men - C & D Coys have now moved to VILLE. Nothing special to report. TBBoyr	
"	9/5/16		The "Batt" found a working party in the morning consisting 200 + 4 officers. Remainder of "Batt" attended Divine Service - The Deputy Chaplain to the Forces taking the Service. In the afternoon the "Batt" played the 10 York & Lancasters Regt at Football drawing 4 - 1. W.E.Thos G.I.Chay	
	10/5/16		Companies placed at disposal of O.C. Coys. Nothing special to report.	

WAR DIARY
or
INTELLIGENCE SUMMARY
(Erase heading not required.)

Army Form C. 2118

Place	Date	Hour	Summary of Events and Information	Remarks and references to Appendices
VILLE	11/4/16		A one day grenade course at which B Coy & Lewis Gun detachment were to take part has to be curtailed on account of the Rain. Companies employed the morning in lectures, instructions & instruction in Gas Helmets drill DF	
	12/4/16		C.O. OC Coys & OC detachments proceeded to visit the Trenches to reconnoitre the ground to be taken over by the Batt'n. The Batt'n forms a working party of 4 Officers & 200 R+F. These were found by A & B Coy leaving Belleurs at Noon by C & D Coy	W.A.D. Mag
	13/4/16		Coys placed at disposal of OC Corps during morning. In afternoon 350 men billets at Bath House 2 Lewis Guns - borrowed from 8 Lincolns. These with Batt' Lewis Guns were sent to S end in the Evening prior to Batt' going into trenches on the following afternoon. Nothing special to report.	
	14/4/16		Battalion relieves the 9th K.O.Y.L.I. in the Trenches. This new sector of the line is in a much worse condition to the Trenches which the Battalion have been in. The enemy is lively & the ground shaky, & therefore things have to dry when trenches must the recovery of Trenches & the enormous quantity of amatol which has to be utilised for that purpose on improvement by their absence. The work of the site however leaves itself to mining enterprise actually fact in duty release by both sides. Relief of units can be (Cotri) TD	

1875 Wt. W593/826 1,000,000 4/15 J.B.C. &A. A.D.S.S./Forms/C.2118.

WAR DIARY or INTELLIGENCE SUMMARY

Army Form C. 2118

Place	Date	Hour	Summary of Events and Information	Remarks and references to Appendices
Trenches near MEAULT & FRICOURT	14/4/16		made during the day owing to the soft & also the hilly rolling nature of the ground. The relief was complete by 6 p.m. The Enemy artillery was active at night here they are able to unearth flares normally & not as in Flanders where the ground was so flat. Our Artillery reply very quietly at all times & reopen in principle to any annoyance from the Enemy. In one Section of the line (See sketch map) the TAMBOOR Rifle Grenades are the chief annoyance & the cause of 80% of our casualties. Our casualties were 1 Killed & 4 wounded the first night owing to this weapon. T.D. Capt.	
"	15/4/16		During morning man killed. The Enemy were again very rich rifle Grenades & Trench Mortars. We replied vigorously both of Artillery & Grenades. Sniping is very scarce here but on Snipers we active & claim 1 hit. Our casualties during day were 1 Killed 1 Wounded. Trench Mortars of 6 Regt taken over by our Heavy Trench Mortar Battery 2.Lieut. HEFFER joined the Battn. T.D. Capt.	
"	16/4/16		A wet day. Enemy firing quiet but intermittent across Tampeveer into his daily shape. There was rather annoying but no offline to water treat. Our casualties during day were 5 wounded T.D. Capt.	

WAR DIARY or INTELLIGENCE SUMMARY

Army Form C. 2118

Place	Date	Hour	Summary of Events and Information	Remarks and references to Appendices
Trenches near MEAULT & FRICOURT.	17/5/16		During day Enemy fairly quiet perhaps owing to the rain. A few rifle grenades were fired by them to which our grenadiers effectively replied silencing them. Our casualties during day were 1 killed & 15 wounded & a Sgt. of 6 a/grenadier joined Bn.	
	18/5/16		Capt Dolan returned from leave. Rifle Grenades & Trench Mortars were busy & we bombarded the enemy trenches at 4 p.m. until 5 p.m. To this he replied & our Casualties during the day were 8 wounded & 2 slightly wounded. T.D.Sgn.	
	19/5/16		The Enemy were more busy during the morning from about 10 a.m. until noon with bombs, grenades, & torpedoes which were nearly all directed on the TAMBOUR. We replied effectively & silenced him temporarily. In this interim rifle grenade went on fire about 250 daily. In the evening at about 6 p.m. the enemy commenced to bombard our firm trenches on the right & also on the steep held by the Bn on our right & last of the Enemy who expected & eagerly awaited by our gunnery replied so effectively on his parapets that the Enemy once out have kept them had to withdraw. In our continued	

WAR DIARY or INTELLIGENCE SUMMARY

Army Form C. 2118

Place	Date	Hour	Summary of Events and Information	Remarks and references to Appendices
Trenches near MEAULT ~ FRICOURT	19/4/16	(contd.)	Obtain the best wind our Artillery kept up its retaliation & eventually all internnes during the night. Our casualties were 1 Killed & 6 wounded. T.B. Baty	about 8.30pm
	20/4/16		Very wet day, little to report. The Div Commr. never trembles. Our Casualties were 2 wounded. T.B. Baty	
	21/4/16		Enemy quiet during morning. Bayts very q. going to observation drawn in the afternoon & evening. Casualties during day nil. T.B. Baty	
	22/4/16		The Bn was relieved by 1st Bn N. Fusiliers commencing at 12.30 p.m. and Signallers the whole Bn being complete by 6.30 p.m. Bn. in billets for the night at VILLE. No Casualties. T.B. Baty	
	23/4/16		Bn paraded at 11am & moved by march route to Div Rest area at Bryans in Div reserve, arriving there at about 2.30pm. The day was very hot but the road being dry about 1 miles was not too irksome for the march. Heavy hail brewing. Billets are good for both Officers. T.B. Baty	

Place	Date	Hour	Summary of Events and Information	Remarks and references to Appendices
LA NEUVILLE	24/4/16		D Coy relieve a 1 Coy came at the Trenches where new Br. trenches & three other coys arranged for the purpose of preparing the attack on lines laid down for probable future operations. Nothing special to report. T.B.Coy.	
	25/4/16		Working parties from G Bn. 500 strong, fr work at Trenches relief. T.B.Coy.	
	26/4/16		Bn. bathed. Coy. at disposal of Bdy. Officers. Gas helmets inspected by Chemical expert. & Strictly pressure on leave. T.B.Coy.	
	27/4/16		Working party of 500 from G Bunker's. Demonstration at noon witnessed by Officers T.B.Coy on to prove the usefulness of German Flammenwerfer. T.B.Coy.	
	28/4/16		A field exercise was carried on by the Battalion the subject being a practice attack across open country. The Bn. has little practice in this sort of warfare but on the whole the exercise was well carried out, the men entering all their energies to the work. Lieut. J. H. Hooper joined the Battalion. T.B.Coy.	
	29/4/16		Divine Service was held at 10.30 a.m. & other ceremonies were attended. Nothing special to report. T.B.Coy.	

Army Form C. 2118

WAR DIARY
or
INTELLIGENCE SUMMARY
(Erase heading not required.)

Instructions regarding War Diaries and Intelligence Summaries are contained in F.S. Regs., Part II. and the Staff Manual respectively. Title Pages will be prepared in manuscript.

Place	Date	Hour	Summary of Events and Information	Remarks and references to Appendices
LA NEUVILLE	30/4/16		Bn Route marched. The Bn football team played the Somerset Lt.Inf. Infantry team & after a most exciting & close game lost 2-1. Having spent to report. T.B.Burge	Lieut Colonel Tommy 4th Bn. Middlesex Regt

Sketch shewing Battalion Front.
April 14-4-16 To 22/4/16

Fricourt.

= Batt. H.Q.
= Co. H.Q.
= Support Co H.Q.

Fricourt Sta.

Cemetery
Crucifix Corner
Rondle Avenue
Kingston Avenue
C Coy
A Coy
B Coy
Sta.
Royal Avenue
Tambour
Tangier
Surrey Street
Kings Ave
Kings Avenue
D Coy
Purfleet

Not to Scale

WAR DIARY or INTELLIGENCE SUMMARY

4 Middlesex Army Form C. 2118

Place	Date	Hour	Summary of Events and Information	Remarks and references to Appendices
LA NUVILLE	May 1st 1916		Battalion route march for 4½ hours, returning 1.30pm. Inspection of feet etc. in the afternoon. A draft of 42 men joined including 1 Sergt & 1 Corporal. Nothing special to report. T.S.Boyd Capt.	
	2/5/16		Battalion fire drill under the Adjutant from 6.45 to 7.30 am. The results were good & a marked increase in steady work. After breakfast the boys were re disposed for training for the practising of the attack on favourite trenches dug near the village. The chief tax to training of the Battalion in extensive formations lies in the lack of experienced general, the desire to train have & do things well is very marked in all ranks & despite the afternoon difficulties must be abundantly & the rush to work have proved most beneficial. The 10th YORK & LANCS & the 8th LINCOLNS moved off to the BRAY-SUR-SOMME area in the early morning. Orders have been given that all ranks when possible are to be exercised before the dawn of the day. Tomorrow we & the 8th Somerset L.I. are to move to VILLE. T.S.Boyd Capt	
VILLE	3/5/16		The Battalion marched to VILLE leaving the LEVEL CROSSING at 6.30 am. The morning was fine & the rain of the previous evening had made the roads good for marching. The Batt arrived at VILLE at 9.30 am. The breech at this place was not very good being narrow in close streets. From this place working parties are to be found daily. 800 in all. Only One humorous were found tonight by the Battalion. T.S.Boyd Capt	
VILLE	4/5/16		On forming working parties. The most serious chiefs of finding Gun emplacements against case invades. Dugouts & a company O.T.s. Two men were wounded by Shrapnel. T.S.Boyd Capt	

Army Form C. 2118

WAR DIARY
or
INTELLIGENCE SUMMARY
(Erase heading not required.)

Instructions regarding War Diaries and Intelligence Summaries are contained in F. S. Regs., Part II. and the Staff Manual respectively. Title Pages will be prepared in manuscript.

Place	Date	Hour	Summary of Events and Information	Remarks and references to Appendices
VILLE SUR SOMME	5/5/16		Working parties found by the battalion. Nothing special to report. TBBayt	
	6/5/16		Working parties as usual. All officers clear of duty attended a demonstration of the AYRTON fan, an apparatus for use with a VERMOREL Sprayer, this at 2 pm near BUIRE. Nothing special to report. TBBayt	
"	7/5/16		Working parties found by battalion. Lt Col BICKNELL proceeded to 4th Army School to attend a 7 days course for senior officers. TBBayt	
"	8/5/16		Working parties as usual. 2Lieut P. BARNETT joined the battalion for duty. 3 wounded. TBBayt	
"	9/5/16		Working parties. Battalion duties. TBBayt	
"	11/5/16		Working parties. Officers reconnoitred the new sector to be taken over tomorrow. Capt O.R.F. JOHNSTON joined & took over command of B Coy. TBBayt	
FRICOURT SECTOR	12/5/16		Battalion relieved the 10th YORKSHIRE REGT in QUEENS REDOUBT, BONTE REDOUBT & in BECORDEL VILLAGE. Battalion Headquarters being at MEAULTE. The battalion is in support to the Battalion holding the front line & the distribution is as follows. TBS / continued	

Army Form C. 2118

WAR DIARY
or
INTELLIGENCE SUMMARY
(Erase heading not required.)

Instructions regarding War Diaries and Intelligence Summaries are contained in F.S. Regs., Part II. and the Staff Manual respectively. Title Pages will be prepared in manuscript.

Place	Date	Hour	Summary of Events and Information	Remarks and references to Appendices
FRICOURT SECTOR.	12/5/16		**STRENGTH** — 2 Officers. 44 Other ranks including 2 approx (1b) Br Bombers	
			Objective — Salient at F.3.C. b.9. 3.6. WICKED CORNER.	
			Objects — To capture Germans To kill Germans To take as much loot as possible To damage Trenches.	
			Reconnaissance — The Officers, N.C.O's & Scouts will reconnoitre the ground between our Trenches & WICKED CORNER every night which was thoroughly reconnoitred and lit.	
			LEWIS GUNS — Lewis Guns of the Battalion holding the line will harass Enemy Trenches on both flanks of the salient (Objective). The Lewis Gun Officer of the raiding battalion superintending making any necessary arrangements with O.C. Lewis armament of the Bn holding the line.	
			Divisional Artillery — Divisional Artillery will concentrate on the salient and figure of cutting wire & destroying M.Gun emplacements & S.E. of it. This wire will take place during hostile bombardment. At a time fixed by Divisional Artillery 2 hours after the Enemy raid a barrage wire be placed behind the objective which will last for 20 minutes. During this time the raid will take place.	The whole in command of 2/Lt St John Jones
			Raiding Parties — Raids will be organised as follows: No. 1 Party — 1 h.6.O. + 7 men (Br. Bombers) " 2 " — 7 " (Bay Bombers) " 3 " — 2 h.6.O. — 10 men — Looting Party. " 4 " — 1 Officer — 7 men — covering party. " 5 " — 1 h.6.O. — 7 men — covering party.	

WAR DIARY or INTELLIGENCE SUMMARY

Army Form C. 2118

Place	Date	Hour	Summary of Events and Information	Remarks and references to Appendices
FRICOURT SECTOR.	1/7/16		Formation for 1 N.C.O. + 2 men (Scouts) from No 5 party. No 1 Party on left & No 2 party on right in single file abreast followed by No 3 & 4 parties in same formation. No 5 party in rear of No 4 accompanied by a stretcher party.	

General Scheme

Enemy
- No 1 Party to prevent along 1st trench running NE about 40 yds to hold it.
- No 2   "   "   "   "   "   "   SE   "   "   "   "
- No 3   "   throw up 2 posts of Communication Trench at point F 3.C.8.9.
- No 4   "   to lead & capture any prisoners across river of Bombing parties. The Officer
- No 5 party (Reserve) close in among parapet at point of Entrance awaiting flanks & this party will cover retirement of raiding party.

Composition of parties

No 1, 2 + 3. will consist of two bayonet men, 2 throwers, 2 scouts, 1 leader + 1 spare man.
No 4 party will carry Rifles & Bayonets fixed (all ladder outlets) + 4 throwers in portion of patrol + one sentry for look.
No 5 Party Rifles & Bayonets fixed, 6 to 8 throwers in rear patrols + a covering for look out.

No Equipment will be worn, steel Helmets will be worn. 10 cartridges + bayonet to be worn, 50 men in front pockets. Throwers carry on Bandoleers containing 10 bombs in their belts containing 10 bombs. All bayonet men to carry one universal bomb. All bombers will carry Belayans.

No 5 party will carry 1 transverse of S.A.A., He & B.O.S. every wheeler & wire cutter. Scouts will also carry wire cutters.

Badges, Gay Books, markings, shiens, gas helmets numbers & all other means of identity will be left behind. An envelope for each man & each wire Regt No & Black mark will be

WAR DIARY
or
INTELLIGENCE SUMMARY

Army Form C. 2118

Place	Date	Hour	Summary of Events and Information	Remarks and references to Appendices
FRICOURT SECTOR	12/5/16		Continued.	

A Coy. - BONTE REDOUBT. The Garrison of this place finds 1 Officer & 80 men for work with miners in Tambour.

B. Coy. - QUEENS REDOUBT. This Garrison also finds a fatigue party daily of 1 Sgt & 30 men for mining work.

C & D Coy. BECORDEL DEFENCES. The Garrison of this village on agreed to find 3 Bn BOMBERS "chips" of 1 Officer & 80 for 8 hours each. These parties in conjunction with A Coy will the 24 hour engineering in near the church. ECOLE-DES GARCONS.

Bn HQrs - MEAULT — The building occupied is near the church. ECOLE-DES GARCONS.

The Companies at BECORDEL have one platoon & 2 squads of BOMBERS always standing by ready to perform a counter-attack on the Enemy trenches should the Enemy enter our. The Company reserve is "C" Coy & 2nd Lt G.A ST-JOHN JONES is O.C of the party with 2Lt H.E. HEFFER assisting him. The names for this party are as follows. In the event of an Enemy raid, this platoon alone is ready to move off via WILLOW AVENUE, KINGSTON AVENUE & ROYAL AVENUE to the SALLY PORT, EAST of the TAMBOUR. The point times for the names in called WICKED CORNER & a road with high banks in each are called the SUNKEN ROAD leads up to this point. (See sketch map).

The signature for this attack are as follows.

B/Baye
Continued

WAR DIARY or INTELLIGENCE SUMMARY

Army Form C. 2118

Place	Date	Hour	Summary of Events and Information	Remarks and references to Appendices
FRICOURT SECTOR	13/6/16		**Intention** Patrol will move free & a white flag will be seen on back in centre of collar as means of identification. **Purpose** Will the raid lead to an Intention & on arrival there all Bowe mining will be taken from then & placed in sandbags. They will then be sent to Battalion Hqrs as soon as the raiding party return. **Stretcher bearers** will stay at Sally Port & persons will ho 5 party & carry in any wounded. If small enemies party will be set up in a disgust men the Sally Port where wounded will be brought, sent to the Regt Aid Post via ROYAL – KINGSTON – WILLOW AVENUES. The moving officer of the raiding Battalion will proceed to Reg Aid Post of the Battalion relieving the line & receive. T.B.Slaupt **Headquarters** The M.O.'s Segment of the relieving Battalion will move to the Hqrs of the Battalion holding the line where report will be sent. T.B.Slaupt The relief was complete by 11pm. There were no casualties. Enemy very quiet. T.B.Slaupt Enemy artillery was active during the day & we effectively retaliated. The 8th Somerset L.I. during the night of 13–14th carried out a minor enterprise which was not a success. No casualties. T.B.Slaupt	

Army Form C. 2118

WAR DIARY
or
INTELLIGENCE SUMMARY
(Erase heading not required.)

Instructions regarding War Diaries and Intelligence Summaries are contained in F.S. Regs., Part II. and the Staff Manual respectively. Title Pages will be prepared in manuscript.

Place	Date	Hour	Summary of Events and Information	Remarks and references to Appendices
FRICOURT SECTOR	14/5/16		Enemy were active during the afternoon from about 2-5 pm but stir later we retaliated. Sgt. Boot Bichnell returned from course at Inf. School. Lieutenant Green was returned from Brigade for trench operations. Battalion operation Green in to proceed to Bray by 3 pm. Number of draft of 112 including 3 Sergts joined the battalion 50% have been out at the front before. There were no casualties during day. T.B.Scarft	
	15/5/16		A quiet day & a lot of aerial activity. Artillery were active during the night chiefly in the vicinity of the TAMBOURS. We sustained no casualties. T.B.Scarft	
	16/5/16		Except for Artillery much nothing seemed to report. In the early morning at about 5.15 the Enemy opened fire with 4.2- the shells landing about 200-300 yards West of MEAULTE CHURCH. They were apparently being searching. About 60% of these shells were blind. No damage was done. The weather is very wet & the glare from the chalk in which the Trenches are dug is rather trying. We sustained one casualty from Rifle Grenades during the day. Wire were again received from 2nd & 13th Battns wishing luck to wear ALBUHERA DAY. T.B.Scarft	ALBUHERA DAY
	17/5/16		Artillery opened to open upon us. We sustained no casualties. T.B.Scarft	
	18/5/16		A lot of Aerial activity & little else. In the evening from about 6-8 pm there was a good deal of Trench mortaring in the vicinity of the TAMBOUR. Our retaliation was effective & silenced them. No casualties. T.B.Scarft	

1875 Wt. W593/826 1,000,000 4/15 J.B.C. & A. A.D.S.S./Forms/C. 2118

Army Form C. 2118

WAR DIARY
or
INTELLIGENCE SUMMARY
(Erase heading not required.)

Instructions regarding War Diaries and Intelligence Summaries are contained in F.S. Regs., Part II. and the Staff Manual respectively. Title Pages will be prepared in manuscript.

Place	Date	Hour	Summary of Events and Information	Remarks and references to Appendices
FRICOURT SECTOR	19/5/16		A very quiet day. Aerial activity & little else. The wind is slight but is in favour of an Enemy Gas enterprise. All ranks were duly warned & precautions taken but nothing relative to Gas happened. It is believed that the Enemy have numerous Gas cylinders in the Boche Trenches as shown by aeroplane photos. There was no casualties during the day.	T.S.Bloye Capt
"	20/5/16		A quiet day with very little Artillery activity. A good day for observation but nothing special to no movement was seen.	T.S.Bloye Capt
"	21/5/16		Artillery active but little retaliation. One man killed by rifle Grenade in the TAMBOUR.	T.S.Bloye Capt
"	22/5/16		Bn relieved by 13th Bn NORTHUMBERLAND FUSILIERS relief being completed by 3.30 pm. Enemy evidently spotted relief & some were knocked about and was sent over fairly freely through MEAULTE but we sustained no casualties. The Bn billeted at BUIRE for the night.	T.S.Bloye Capt
BUIRE	23/5/16		The Bn paraded for the march to LA NEUVILLE at 8 A.M. The route via TREUX, MÉRICOURT & CORBIE – a distance of about 8 miles. On	

Army Form C. 2118

WAR DIARY
or
INTELLIGENCE SUMMARY
(Erase heading not required.)

Instructions regarding War Diaries and Intelligence Summaries are contained in F. S. Regs., Part II. and the Staff Manual respectively. Title Pages will be prepared in manuscript.

Place	Date	Hour	Summary of Events and Information	Remarks and references to Appendices
LA NEUVILLE	23/5/16		The whole the Battalion marched well & arrived at LA NUEVILLE at about 11.30 a.m. The same front billets were occupied as before. Coy Comms were abolished & Coy Police instituted. T/Blakop	
	24/5/16		Coy parade for training in wood fighting at ESCARDONNEUSE WOOD T after an inspection moving returned to billets at 12.30 p.m. The afternoon was devoted to inspections. T/Blakop	
	25/5/16		A Brigade Tactical exercise was arranged to test plan trying to test the best means of desperate co-operation with infantry in the attack. Owing to the weather it has to be postponed. Coy and cheps at the disposal of Coy Commanders. T/Blakop	
	26/5/16		During the morning two Coys carried out Bomb throwing practice & all held a ½ H A & C who have not thrown live bombs out as & other Coy practice under supervision of the Brigade Bombing Officer with Dummy Bombs, & also practice the attack on the Facenille Trenches near LA NEUVILLE. These exercises are being used to foster the offensive spirit in all ranks which is apt to overcome in his Trench Warfare which has lasted so long. T/Blakop	

Army Form C. 2118

WAR DIARY or INTELLIGENCE SUMMARY

(Erase heading not required.)

Place	Date	Hour	Summary of Events and Information	Remarks and references to Appendices
LA NEUVILLE	27/5/16		Batt. practised the attack in conjunction with the 10th YORK & LANCS who are our supporting battalion in case of future operations. A lecture on trench warfare was held in the evening to all Officers & Senior Officers, the new Divisional commander being Brig. Gen. D.G.M. Campbell who has succeeded Gen. Ingouville Williams. The General Officer being present.	
	28/5/16		Divine Service was held for all denominations, the B.G.O.E. service being held in the further field. Nothing special to report. T.B.Cooper	
	29/5/16		The Engineers attacked which was postponed on the 25th inst. was carried out. The scheme was to follow up Stokes' and artillery made action on ground & trenches before our successive waves & their role was to report commencement of progress & any movements or further counter attack upon the enemy & of the results of our bombardment & when to advance. The course of aeroplanes was arranged so as to witness the positions was a success although it is difficult to judge whether when were bombarded whatever firing they [illegible] were to penetrate. The scheme was most instructive to the usual, were carried out. In the evening a Brigade Boxing Tournament took place, some excellent fights were witnessed. The Battalion were well represented & put up some very good fights & were also well represented in the prize list. T.B.Cooper	

WAR DIARY
or
INTELLIGENCE SUMMARY

Army Form C. 2118.

(Erase heading not required.)

Instructions regarding War Diaries and Intelligence Summaries are contained in F. S. Regs., Part II. and the Staff Manual respectively. Title Pages will be prepared in manuscript.

Place	Date	Hour	Summary of Events and Information	Remarks and references to Appendices
LA NEUVILLE	30/5/16		Corps practices Bombing etc at the Practice Trenches & also phases of the attack. A football match resulting in a draw was played by an officers & the 8th LINCOLNS the men being O—O. — T.B.Capt	
	31/5/16		The Divisional Commander inspected the Brigade at 9.30 a.m. & expressed himself as highly pleased with the Battalion. Transport & the O.C. & other Battalions were allowed up to examine the example of excellence & recommend it on its line. After inspecting the Brigade again practised the attack due without aeroplane observation. The stay at LA NEUVILLE has greatly benefited the troops & we made an appreciable extra charge, for a true espirit-de-corps. A draft of 42 Gunners & 35 Officers Lieut SAPTE reejoined the Battalion from Brigade & Lt Col BICKNELL returned on leave & Major WA ODLING took over command of the Battalion. The Bn moved to MEAULTE tomorrow. — T.B.Capt	

A.W. Odling Major
Commanding 9th Hampshires Regt

O.O. No 5 S E C R E T.

OPERATION ORDER BY

LIEUT-COLONEL H. P. F. BICKNELL, D.S.O.,

COMMANDING, 4TH BATTALION MIDDLESEX REGIMENT.

NOTE.
    Zero is the hour of assault.
    Z day is the day of assault.
    Days previous to the assault
    are allotted a day of the
    alphabet: i.e. U day is the
    5th day before the assault.

MAP REFERENCE:- 1:10,000.

1.   63rd Infantry Brigade O.O. No 58 and 21st Division O.O. No 55 and the Appendixes attached have been explained to all.

2.   Further orders will be issued as to moving into trenches prior to assault.

3.   Communication trenches will be used as follows:-

    UP.
      LINDUM STREET.   HUNTLY STREET.

    DOWN.
      KING'S AVENUE.   QUEEN'S AVENUE.   STONEHAVEN STREET.

    4th Battalion Middlesex Regiment will be responsible for policing KING'S AVENUE, LINDUM STREET and QUEEN'S AVENUE. Parties for this purpose will be detailed later, and special instructions issued to them.

4. ASSEMBLY AREA.
    Brigade Headquarters at Junction of 101 STREET and SHUTTLE LANE. 4th Bn Middlesex Regiment Headquarters near Brigade Headquarters.
    "A" Company in front trench from F. 2 b 8580 to board marked "GUILDFORD" "X 26/1".
    "B" Company from "GUILDFORD" "X 26/1" to point in new trench 50 yards North of where it joins the present front line.
    "C" Company two Platoons in 104a STREET and old front trench, and two Platoons in LINDUM STREET.
    "D" Company. in SHUTTLE LANE between junction of 101 STREET and 104a STREET.
    Battalion Grenadiers (less 1 squad) in SHUTTLE LANE on the left of "D" Company and the remainder at Battalion Headquarters in SHUTTLE LANE on the right of "D" Company.

5.   The 4th Middlesex Regiment on the right, 8th Somerset Light Infantry on left will deliver the assault on first objective.

6.
(a) 1ST OBJECTIVE.
    The 4th Middlesex Regiment will seize and consolidate FRICOURT FARM X 28 c 8.7 and bend of trench X 28 a 5005 inclusive with advanced posts in RAILWAY ALLEY and RAILWAY COPSE up to RAILWAY LINE about X 28 b 1.3 inclusive.

    8th Bn Somerset Light Infantry from bend of trench at X 28 a 5005 exclusive. CRUCIFIX TRENCH to X 27 b 7841 with advanced posts from X 28 b 1.3 exclusive to S. end of SHELTER WOOD exclusive.

(b) 2ND OBJECTIVE.
    10th York & Lancs Regiment X 29 b 5.6. (joining up with 7th Division Thence along Northern edge of BOTTOM WOOD by Works 16/13 to new trench X 29 a 1.8 along new trench to QUADRANGLE TRENCH X 23 c 4.5 (exclusive). The following advanced line will be occupied at once and consolidated as soon as the main objective has been consolidated --- X 29 b 5.6 --- Work 17 QUADRANGLE WOOD to Work 18 -- X 23 d.0548.

    8th Bn Lincolnshire Regiment (see sheet No m 2.)

(Sheet 2.)

8th Lincoln Regiment X 23 d 1500-QUADRANGLE to X 23 c 6565 (where QUADRANGLE trench crosses MAMETZ-CONTALMAISON ROAD) inclusive with advanced posts on the line X 23 d 6.0 RAILWAY to X 23 d 2590.

7. The dividing line between 4th Middlesex Regiment and 8th Somerset Light Infantry to the first objective will be a line drawn from the point of junction in the assembly trench to the EASTERN end of LOZENGE WOOD and from there to point X 28 a 5005.

BOUNDARIES The dividing line between 4th Middlesex Regiment and 50th Infantry Brigade (10th W.Yorks Regt) will be a line drawn from point of junction in assembly trenches to X 27 c 30.25--X 27 d 0542 from the latter point the right flank of "A" Company will be directed on the S.E. of FRICOURT FARM enclosure.

The dividing line between "A" & "B" Companies will be a line from the point of junction in assembly trench LONELY LANE (inclusive to right Company) and thence to trench junction X 28 c 8.7.

The general bearing of the line of advance is 92 degrees magnetic.

8. "C" Company will detail two Sections and two Lewis Guns to consolidate and hold the trench running East from X 27 d 1.5. Officer in charge of Battalion Grenadiers will detail one squad to accompany this party: this squad will join "C" Company in assembly trenches.

This party will remain till ordered to join their Company, but the Lewis Guns will rejoin when relieved by Machine Gun Company.

"C" Company will also consolidate the Southern and Eastern edges of FRICOURT FARM enclosure, and block trenches leading to FRICOURT WOOD. The Battalion Grenadier Officer will be prepared to block RAILWAY ALLEY and the trenches running N.E. & S.W. from X 28 c 88.

9. The 50th Infantry Brigade is attacking simultaneously on the right with the object of clearing the front system of German trenches and protecting the right flank of the 63rd Infantry Brigade.

10. Two Companies specially detailed for the purpose will follow immediately behind the assaulting Battalion's to clear the German trenches.

11. On reaching the first objective the leading Companies will be responsible for pushing forward the advanced posts and consolidating the line.

12. Two Stokes Mortars will follow behind the rear Company and will be available for use against any point.

13. Five minutes before Zero the leading lines of assaulting Battalions will leave their trenches and creep forward as close to the German trenches as our barrage permits.

The second lines will also leave their trenches and lie down close to the leading lines. Should the hostile fire not permit of this the assault will be started from our front line.

14. Packs will not be carried.

220 rounds S.A.A., 2 sandbags, and 2 grenades per man will be carried.

Also 150 picks and 150 shovels:- The two leading Platoons of the two leading Platoons will not xx carry these tools.

All the above will be drawn at VILLE.

Gas Helmets will be worn rolled up on the head.

On leaving the assembly area Battalion Headquarters will be established near X 27 d 1555 and on moving forward from here X 28 c 8.8.

Regimental Aid Posts are on sheet 3.

(Sheet 3.).

16. Regimental Aid Posts are established at

    4th Bn Middlesex Regiment ......Junction.

    8th Somerset Light Infantry........Junction of QUEENS AVENUE and SURREY STREET.

    10th York & Lancs Regt............Junction of QUEENS AVENUE and SURREY STREET.

    8th Lincoln Regt..................Junction of MARISCHALL STREET and STONEHAVEN STREET.

17. The following Battalion reserve of ammunition etc will be stored behind the assembly trenches and will be carried forward by the two rear Platoons of "D" Company.

    S.A.A......20,000.

    Lewis Guns.....192, Drums.

    Grenades......1,000.

A Brigade reserve will be carried forward by 62nd Infantry Brigade and dumped in the SUNKEN ROAD.

                                      Signed

                                      T.L.BODEN, Captain,

Adjutant, 4th Battalion Middlesex Regiment.

CERTIFIED A TRUE COPY OF ORIGINAL BATTALION OPERATION ORDER-

                                      2/Lieutenant,

a/Adjutant, 4th Battalion Middlesex Regiment.

WAR DIARY
or
INTELLIGENCE SUMMARY

Army Form C. 2118.

4 Middlesex

Place	Date	Hour	Summary of Events and Information	Remarks and references to Appendices
MEAULTE	June 1st		The Battalion marched out of LA NEUVILLE at 6.30 a.m. en route to MEAULTE when we are to be under the command of the 11th Brigade for working parties & receiving fatigue purposes. The day was very hot & straining to a great number than is usual and the Battalion fell out. They all however eventually rejoined at MEAULTE - which place was reached at about 11 a.m. Disposition of the Battalion as follows:- A Coy at VILLE B Coy on the INTERMEDIARY LINE C } MEAULTE D } Bn. Headquarters MEAULTE. Working parties are found by the Battalion for work under R.E supervision in and nearby vicinity of Dugout & Emplacement construction. The Coy in the INTERMEDIARY LINE are employed on the execution of strong points along this line & these posts are numbered from right to left 15-20. During the three days we working parties were from 6 am	
	June 2nd		Consistently any heavy attack in case employ on making fire & revetting the trench. Enemy attempted raid on our left at 2h about to came to about an hour after this time the enemy flashed out & all returned to trench. We occasioned considerable enemy fires of A.Coy, 1 killed 3 wounded	

WAR DIARY
INTELLIGENCE SUMMARY

Army Form C. 2118.

Place	Date	Hour	Summary of Events and Information	Remarks and references to Appendices
MEAULTE	3rd/6/16		Nothing of special interest. The Enemy were rather offensive during the afternoon & shelled the environs of MEAULTE causing some casualties to a battalion of the K.O.Y.L.I. but none to us. About 80 shells arrived got about 4·5 calibre — our artillery retaliated on CONTALMAISON which place we suspect is the same manner. At the Enemy the village & the shelling of took orders holding sent there as a hostility for the other, & it either place is fired on the opposing village receives a very prompt reply. It is thought at least for the present, to leave well alone. We suffered no casualties during the day. On this area the Kings birthday honours were published in the London Gazette. The Commanding Officer Lt. Col. BICKNELL receiving the D.S.O. Capt T.S. WOLLOCOMBE (now with the 11th Bn) receiving the MILITARY CROSS & Sergt J. WALKER (signal Sergt) receiving the MILITARY MEDAL. T.S.B. Capt.	These honours were recommended about MARCH last
	4/6/16		The Artillery on both sides were fairly active during the day & there was a fair amount of aerial activity. It rained in places & took place at about 11 pm of the last LINCOLN REGT. The Enemy was apparently surprised at & promptly after dark he sweeps a barrage along the whole of our front. Our Artillery were very active & for quite two hours the bombardment of both sides was continuous. It	

Army Form C. 2118.

WAR DIARY
or
INTELLIGENCE SUMMARY
(Erase heading not required.)

Place	Date	Hour	Summary of Events and Information	Remarks and references to Appendices
MEAULTE	4/9/16		Were thought highly probable that the Enemy were about to attack & therefore drew companies from MEAULTE (C & D Coy) moved up to the INTERMEDIARY LINE occupying Pr 19 & 20 posts. The raid which has been planned could not take place. It is believed that on its left the Enemy were about then trenches but he did not get across "NO MANS LAND". At about 1.30 A.M. (5th) normal withdrawn was resumed & at 2.30 AM completed. C & D Coys returned to billets. We sustained no casualties. T.B.Bleap	
	5/9/16		The usual Working Parties found by the Battalion. A quiet day on our front. Nothing special to report. No casualties. T.B.Bleap	
	6/9/16		A wet stormy & dull miserable day, a little shelling rising to evening but nothing of import to report. T.B.Bleap. Strength of 12 officers the Battalion T.B.Bleap	
	7/9/16		Working parties as report. Enemy artillery fairly active. The following officers join for duty. 2Lieut T.B.Bleap	
	8/9/16		Normal Working parties. Nothing important to comment. T.B.Bleap	

Army Form C. 2118.

WAR DIARY
or
INTELLIGENCE SUMMARY
(Erase heading not required.)

Instructions regarding War Diaries and Intelligence Summaries are contained in F. S. Regs., Part II. and the Staff Manual respectively. Title Pages will be prepared in manuscript.

Place	Date	Hour	Summary of Events and Information	Remarks and references to Appendices
MEAULTE	9/6/16		During the morning the Commanding Officer & all other Company Commanders the Trenches in the Sector allotted out is to occupy. The remainder of the Trenches were employed the TAMBOUR in Rear. The Enemy were rather during the morning not Trench however which seemed to come from ? the Trenches have experience will. A lot of work will be required to keep these Trenches in a defensible state. On the evening LT COL DIETNELL. DSO. Reprimand from Trans & took over command of the Section. T.B.Bleap.	
FRICOURT SECTOR [crossed out]	10/6/16		Working Parties were found by the Battalion as usual. Enemy were remarkably quiet. A few shells fell South of the village. Rain fell during the day preventing much activity. No Casualties. T.B.Bleap.	
MEAULTE				
FRICOURT SECTOR	11/6/16		The Battalion relieved the 15th Durham Light Infantry in the Trenches of the Right Sector of the Divisional Front. The Disposition of the Battalion were as follows. D Coy on the Right } Firing C Coy on Left - Firing Line (TAMBOUR) A " in Centre } Line B " in Support Bn Hive in RAVINE. T.B.Bleap (Commdr.)	

Army Form C. 2118.

WAR DIARY
or
INTELLIGENCE SUMMARY

(Erase heading not required.)

Place	Date	Hour	Summary of Events and Information	Remarks and references to Appendices
FRICOURT SECTOR.	11/6/16		Summary. Relief was completed by 11 AM. No casualties recurred during the relief. Two Riflemen taken during the day by Trench Mortar fire. Enemy had one party within during the early part of the night & also during the day when on dangerous parties were out on dangerous forays near. Our Snipers claim one hit. Transport were heard in direction of FRICOURT about 9.30pm. The enemy chief emmr-of emergene has now is that of a Trench Mortar which fires a Canister of about 8" calibre which explodes with a deafening retornation. It effects are very local but very nervenskating. Our heavy howitzers effectually dealt with this source of emergene & about 40 rounds of 8" or one of these Mortar emplacements. Patrols were busy along the whole of our Front but except for a wiring party near the TAMBOUR had nothing to report. Our Lewis Guns sent this party & dispersed them. T.B.Baup	
	12/6/16		Leow H.Q. fire than usual. Our Snipers claim no hits. A wiring party was seen & dispersed by our rifle fire. The Enemy Artillery were very offensive against the TAMBOUR & the Centre Coy; and Rifle Grenades. Air Contact was to fire a Canister & two grenades on each side, endeavy to prevent dodging & this was certainly work well to army. Our Artillery & Trench Mortar Officers replied promises them eventually. Our Casualties were 1 wounded & 1 slightly wounded. T.B.Baup	

Army Form C. 2118.

WAR DIARY or INTELLIGENCE SUMMARY

(Erase heading not required.)

Place: FRICOURT SECTOR.

Date	Hour	Summary of Events and Information	Remarks
13/6/16		A victory & bad for trenches. Enemy mortars were again busy in front of our Trenches near PONT DE BUSSY who employing them in. TANGIER & KINGS AVENUE also came in for attention. Our Artillery again this am excellent shooting & succeeded in knocking them. A patrol under Lieut A. BRANCH went out for the purpose of capturing one of the Enemy in the identification in regimen. No success was met with. We had no casualties during the day. T.D.Cooper	
14/6/16		Enemy again quiet & his mortars did not fire at all. The chief annoyance during the day were his 7.7's & 5.9 g.m. which was firing at the rate of 1 round every 3 minutes probably the whole daylight. The shooting was poor & many of the rounds were duds. Queens Redoubt, Bécourt & Survey Street received most of the attention from this gun. Sahibs went out at about 9.45 pm in the vicinity of the crater Lieut seven Lieut ST JOHN gave out along our whole front. A patrol from C Coy men. They were opposed by a German listening post on left of the Crater & fired upon all of the patrol lay low except an Officer who ran to the right to take up a position where he could protect the flank & also to obtain information that the above mentioned	

Place	Date	Hour	Summary of Events and Information	Remarks and references to Appendices
FRICOURT SECTOR	14/6/16		2/Lieut was missing. After waiting for about 2 hrs the patrol went out to look for him. They took a different route to another portion of the enemy in a cap & were fired upon at point blank range. 2/Lieut St John Jones is believed to have been killed. Several patrols went out even to find his body but it was not there. It is thought that whether killed or wounded the enemy took him to reinforce their purpose. 2/Lieut Burgen (who was the 2/Lieut's host) was not found & no trace of him was seen. 2/Lieut Schell went out & those of our men with no enemy patrol. Our Casualties during the day were 2/Lieut St John Jones — missing & also 2/Lieut Burgen, & one slightly wounded. Our shelling was some excellent firing in retaliation to Enemy minnen & affording alarmen zum. There — was no special activity. 2/Lieut Burgen came in at night. The strength of this h.Q. is nearly to give. Casualties were	
	15/6/16			

T.B. Capt

Army Form C. 2118.

WAR DIARY
or
INTELLIGENCE SUMMARY
(Erase heading not required.)

Instructions regarding War Diaries and Intelligence Summaries are contained in F. S. Regs., Part II. and the Staff Manual respectively. Title Pages will be prepared in manuscript.

Place	Date	Hour	Summary of Events and Information	Remarks and references to Appendices
Fricourt Sector	16/6/16		The Enemy was quiet but our Artillery which has been swelled enormously after our trenches. The 8th LINCOLN Regt relieves the Battalion by 11 a.m. & we moved into Bde reserve at MEAULTE went on fatigue at QUEENS REDOUBT for carrying purposes. No casualties. T B Bloor	
Meaulte	17/6/16		The whole of the Battalion stayed in Bivouac. Working parties were unknown for working period. There was our usual activity for working parties before the B/n fell in. No casualties. 2 Lieut. A Burch joined the B/n for duty. T B Bloor	
Meaulte	18/6/16		The CEO & all day Commrs made the trenches as a reconnaisance connected with future operations. Working party as usual. Nothing of note to report. No casualties. T B Bloor	

Army Form C. 2118.

WAR DIARY
or
INTELLIGENCE SUMMARY
(Erase heading not required.)

Instructions regarding War Diaries and Intelligence Summaries are contained in F. S. Regs., Part II. and the Staff Manual respectively. Title Pages will be prepared in manuscript.

Place	Date	Hour	Summary of Events and Information	Remarks and references to Appendices
MEAULTE	19/6/16		Working parties were provided by Battalion. Nothing special to report. No casualties. T.B. Clapp	
	20/6/16		Bn relieved by 13th Durham Lgt Infantry, relief being completed at noon. Bn marched to VILLE where dinners were ready. After dinner the Bn marched to LA NEUVILLE. Enemy was busy shelling the Kite Balloon which is stationed at VILLE until the reach that several shells fell unpleasantly near the Battalion. The journey we encountered no casualties. We arrived at LA NEUVILLE at about 5pm. Billets meagre & clean. T.B. Clapp	
LA NEUVILLE	21/6/16 22/6/16 23/6/16		During the stay of the Battalion here men are to have as much rest as possible. In view of the coming offensive operation (see O.O. which is attached) all ranks are to be kept as fit as possible. Sports are held daily between & everything seems to promote "esprit de corps". The men are looking very fit & are	

2449 Wt. W14957/M90 750,000 1/16 J.B.C. & A. Forms/C.2118/12.

Army Form C. 2118.

Instructions regarding War Diaries and Intelligence Summaries are contained in F. S. Regs., Part II. and the Staff Manual respectively. Title Pages will be prepared in manuscript.

WAR DIARY
or
INTELLIGENCE SUMMARY
(Erase heading not required.)

Place	Date	Hour	Summary of Events and Information	Remarks and references to Appendices
LA NEUVILLE	21st to 23rd 6/16		Quiet. Men eager to get to grips with the Enemy, & Brigade friction arm carries out one day mid-day results. attached T.B.Bloop	
	23 to 25th 6/16		Having spent to repair. Everyone preparing for the Great Offensive. All looking any fr. The Bombardment is maximum on the 24th. Orders common on the 25th fr. anty. Lieut. S. MIRIAMS given the O. fr anty T.B.Bloop	

WAR DIARY
or
INTELLIGENCE SUMMARY

Army Form C. 2118.

Place	Date	Hour	Summary of Events and Information	Remarks and references to Appendices
LA HEUVILLE	26/6/16	7.30 p.m.	Battalion proceeded to VILLE en route to Trenches, foyer	OFFICERS [illegible list of officer names]
VILLE	27/6/16	9 p.m.	Battalion moved to enemy line (new O.O.) arriving there 2-30 a.m. 28/6. Subsequent bombardment was in progress during which we lost 3 O.R. killed & 7 wounded. 28/6/16	
LEFT SECTOR	28/6/16	7 p.m.	Orders were received that the assault where we were to have taken place next morning had been postponed for 48 hours. The B[illegible] proceeded L.J. took over the whole of the Brigade front line to [illegible] with [illegible] trenches & Queen Street which only remained until 9-30 p.m. 30 [illegible] 29/6 [illegible]	
QUEEN'S ROUGH	29/6/16	—		
LEFT SECTOR	30/6/16	—	Battalion again went into their own line trenches, disposition as before & still in [illegible]. During the [illegible] of our own wire, 2/Lt Sykes (Capt. J.E.Jordan) was wounded & [illegible] Sgts. [illegible] took over as [illegible] Sutulning bombardment still in progress	

30/6/16
F. Tuthill, Lt Col

Re L/Cpl Burgess reported Missing, 14th inst.

To

Headquarters,

63rd Infantry Brigade.
....

No 7332 Lance-Corporal Burgess states:-
" At about 9-45pm on 14th inst, I volunteered to go on Patrol with 2nd Lieut G.A.St John Jones. We were 4 in all and the officer. We passed along the lip of the left crater, and then came upon a German Sap on left of crater. Whilst there one of the enemy put up a Very Light and saw us. He opened fire and I got up and ran to the right in direction of craters, and there I lay behind a big piece of chalk. The remainder of the Patrol remained where they were. After I had been there for about two minutes. I saw one of the enemy approaching me. He was walking. When he had arrived within about 5 yards of me, I at once fired and he fell, and was I think killed.
At this moment two of the enemy came from my left and knocked the rifle out of my hand, and pointed to my equipment, and told me by motions to take it off. I did so. One of them carried my equipment, and another my rifle towards their own trench.
On arrival at their trench which was very narrow the leading German got into the trench, I got on to the edge of the trench on my knees to climb into it. The other German came unto my left, and was standing on the edge of the trench. I grabbed hold of his legs and pulled him over into the trench. I then jumped up and ran. I ran in the direction of one of the craters, and met another patrol who threw bombs at me. I then went back along the lip of the crater and by this time I had lost my bearings. I walked and crawled about NO MANS LAND for about four hours, and eventually I saw a shell crater and got into it as it was getting light, I remained there all day.
I could hear a lot of shouting during the day, and knew that I was close to the German trench.
I rejoined our lines at night on the left of the TAMBOUR, I crawled through our wire, and looked over the parapet and saw my own C.S.M. The enemy made no attempt to shoot me, and was evidently looking for a captive alive.
I did not see what happened to the officer after I had left the Patrol, I did not see him again.

CERTIFIED A TRUE COPY OF THE ORIGINAL.

2nd Lieutenant,

a/Adjutant, 4th Battalion Middlesex Regiment.

16-6-16.

www.ingramcontent.com/pod-product-compliance
Lightning Source LLC
Chambersburg PA
CBHW081555160426
43191CB00011B/1932